# HOW 2

PETER ELDIN

Illustrated by David Farris

**PUBLISHED IN ASSOCIATION WITH SCOTTISH TV AND PRIMETIME**

RESEARCHED BY: ANDY PRENDERGAST, JUDY PREECE & KATHERINE GRINSTEAD

PRODUCERS: TIM EDMUNDS & ADRIAN EDWARDS

EXECUTIVE PRODUCER: J. NIGEL PICKARD

DIRECTOR: JEREMY CROSS



Hodder & Stoughton

A MEMBER OF THE HODDER HEADLINE GROUP

**How 2**

*British Library Cataloguing in Publication Data*

Eldin, Peter
"How 2"
I. Title
032

ISBN 0 340 60270 8

First published 1993

| Impression number | 10 9 | 8 | 7 | 6 | 5 | 4 | 3 |
|---|---|---|---|---|---|---|---|
| Year | 1998 | 1997 | | 1996 | | 1995 | 1994 |



Typeset by Litho Link Ltd, Welshpool, Powys.
Printed in Great Britain for the educational publishing division of Hodder & Stoughton Ltd. Mill Road, Dunton Green, Sevenoaks, Kent TN13 2YA by Cox & Wyman Ltd, Reading.

# HOW 2 SURVIVE THIS BOOK!

This book is packed with amazing facts and fantastic tricks and activities. You will be able to do most of the tricks and activities on your own but when you see the symbol below, you should get a grown-up to help you.

Although some of the tricks involve the use of dead matches and matchboxes, do remember never to play with live matches.

**Above all take care and have fun!**

# CONTENTS

# HOW CAN YOU MAKE MONEY DISAPPEAR?

1 Say to a friend, 'If I can make some of your money disappear before your very eyes, can I keep it?'. If your friend is foolish enough to accept, borrow a coin and place it on a table.

2 Now place a glass tumbler on top of the coin. Your friend will be quite confident that the cash will not be lost as it can still be seen.

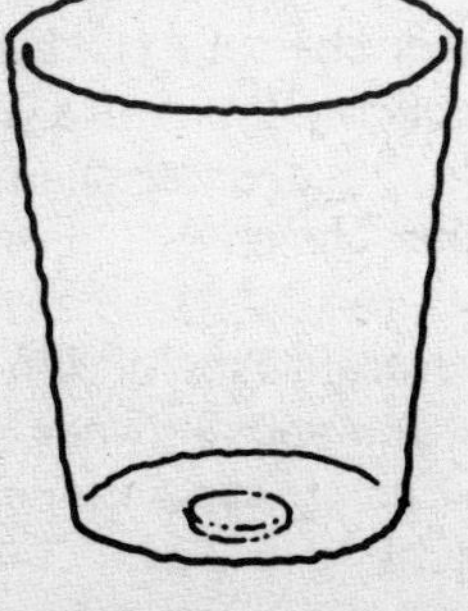

3 Next take a jug of water and pour it into the glass.

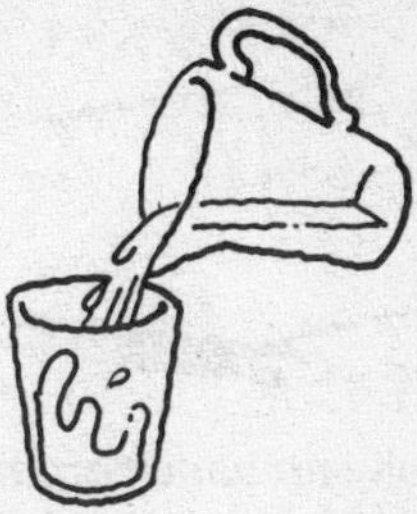

4 Much to everyone's complete and utter astonishment – the coin vanishes!

Actually the coin is still under the glass but it can't be seen. It's not magic, it's science. The water is bending the light so that you can't see the coin. If you don't believe this, place a pencil into a bowl of water. As it goes into the water it appears to bend – that is what is happening to make the coin disappear.

# HOW RUDE IS A PIECE OF PAPER?

YOU CAN CAUSE A PIECE OF PAPER TO MAKE RATHER A RUDE NOISE.

1 Take a sheet of paper and place a pencil on one corner.

2 Roll the paper around the pencil, then hold it in place with a piece of sticky tape.

3 Tip out the pencil, leaving yourself with a paper tube.

4 Cut one end so that it looks like an arrow head, as shown.

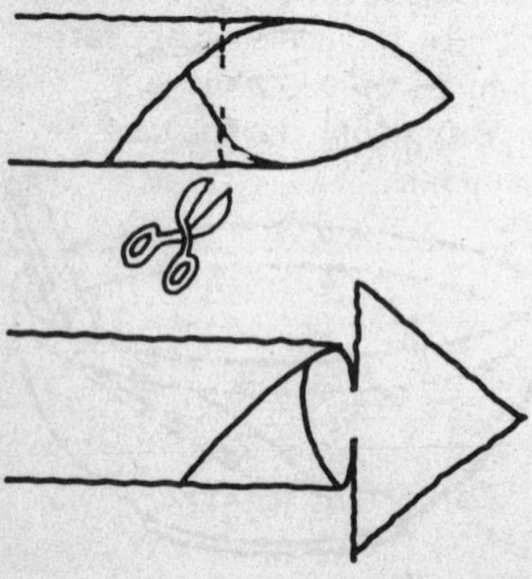

5 Now fold the arrow shape down to cover the end of the tube.

6 Place the other end of the tube in your mouth and suck. The noise you make should be very rude indeed!

The longer the tube the lower the raspberry-type note you produce. The shorter the tube the higher the note.

Make several tubes of different lengths and you and your friends can create a raspberry orchestra!

# HOW CATS HELPED BRITAIN WIN THE WAR

AT THE BACK OF A CAT'S EYE IS A SURFACE THAT REFLECTS LIGHT.

The cat's eyes you see on roads copy this reflective action. They were invented by a Yorkshireman, Percy Shaw, shortly before the start of the Second World War. They consist of two lenses held in a rubber mounting. When placed in the road they reflect the light from a car's headlights so that the driver can see where he or she is going.

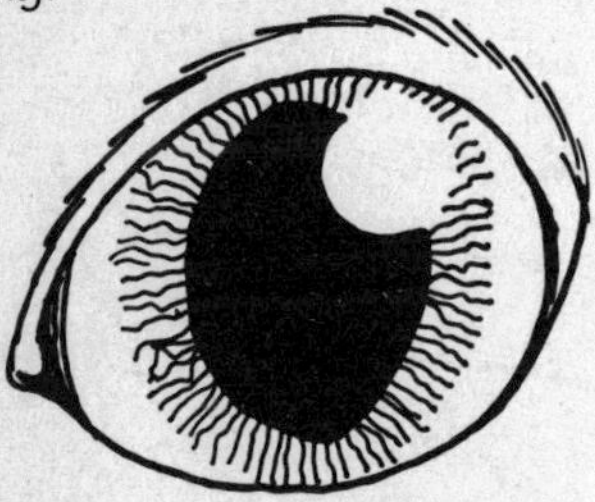

During the war it was absolutely vital that all lights were turned out so that bombers flying overhead at night could not see where they were dropping their bombs.

However, it was also vital that cars and military vehicles moving about at night could see where they were going. Car headlamps were fitted with covers in which there were small hooded slits. Although these did prevent the aeroplanes overhead spotting vehicles, it also meant that the driver was unable to see where he or she was going. However, they did cast enough light to light up cat's eyes, so these were put into the roads to solve the problem.

So that's how cat's eyes helped Britain win the Second World War and how cat's eyes have helped drivers at night ever since.

# HOW CAN YOU COOK FROZEN ICE-CREAM?

IT SOUNDS HARD TO BELIEVE THAT YOU CAN TAKE FROZEN ICE-CREAM OUT OF A BOILING HOT OVEN WITHOUT THE ICE-CREAM MELTING, BUT IT CAN BE DONE.

**YOU WILL NEED:** a block of ice-cream, 3 eggs, 6 oz (150 g) caster sugar, a swiss roll.

1 The secret is to wrap the ice-cream in its own heat-proof jacket made from meringue. To make meringue you need the whites of three eggs.
To separate the whites from the yolks, crack the eggs open against the side of a bowl and then tip the yolk from one half of the shell to the other and back again a few times. The yolk remains in the shell but all of the white goes into the bowl. Check that there is no yolk in the bowl or the meringue will not work. (Keep the yolks for other cooking.)

2 Beat the egg-whites until they are quite stiff. The secret of successful meringue is lots of air and the beating gets the air into the whites. Now fold in the sugar. Do this very gently or you will bash out all the air and your heat-proof jacket will not work.

3 **T**he bottom part of the heat-proof jacket is slices of swiss roll. This is full of air as well to protect your ice-cream from the heat. Place the slices of swiss roll on a baking tray.

4 **P**ut a block of ice-cream on top. Cover the whole lot with the meringue mixture, spreading it evenly all over the top and sides of the ice-cream and sponge. Make sure that there are no holes or thin areas in the meringue or the ice-cream will melt when you put it into the oven.

5 **N**ow put it into a hot oven (450 degrees F/230 degrees C/Gas Mark 8) for three or four minutes. When you take it out the meringue will be crispy and the ice-cream will still be frozen.

# HOW DID THE MAD HATTER GET HIS NAME?

The Mad Hatter is a famous character from Lewis Carroll's book *Alice's Adventures in Wonderland*, which he wrote in 1865. 'As mad as a hatter' is also a popular saying.

But why are hatters said to be mad?

It is because in the past mercury was used to make the felt from which hats were made. Mercury is very poisonous and if repeatedly handled can be slowly absorbed into the human body. It can cause a loss of co-ordination, upsets balance and affects vision. It is no wonder that people thought hat-makers were mad.

# HOW DO FISH GO UP AND DOWN?

Fish can move up and down in the water because of their very clever design.

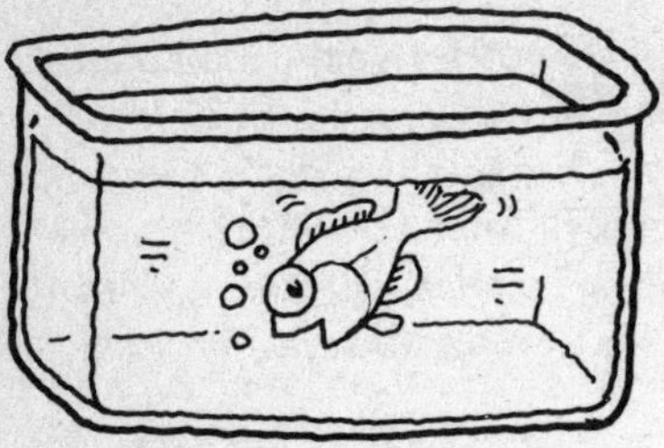

If fish were designed like ping-pong balls, they would float on the surface all the time. If they were designed like stones, they would just sink to the bottom. But many fish have inside them a balloon-like structure called a swim-bladder.

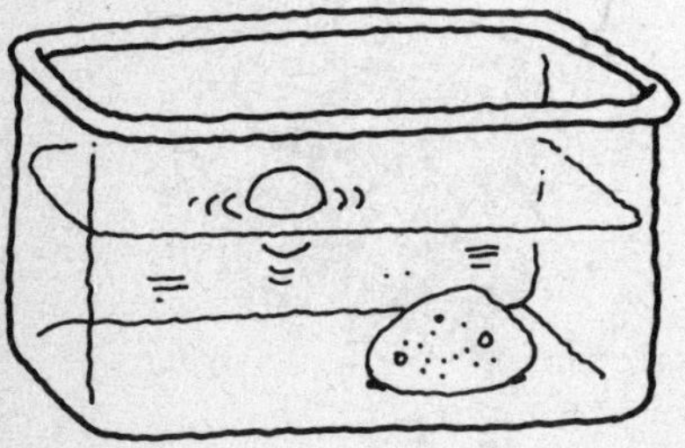

The swim-bladder is full of gases. When the fish wants to go down, it releases some of these gases. When it wants to go up, it increases the amount of gas in the swim-bladder.

Not all fish have swim-bladders. Some have to move up and down in the water by the strength of their muscles alone.

You can make a sort of swim-bladder with a plastic bottle full of water and a small eye dropper. Put the eye dropper in the bottle and then put the bottle cap back on. If you squeeze the bottle you compress the air in the eye dropper and it sinks to the bottom. By releasing your grip the eye dropper can be made to return to the surface.

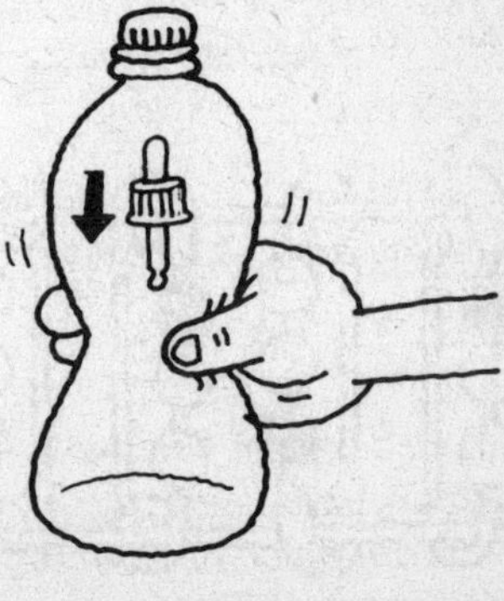

# HOW GLAMOROUS IS A SAFETY PIN?

YOU MIGHT NOT THINK THAT A SAFETY PIN IS VERY GLAMOROUS. BUT THE SIMPLE SAFETY PIN CAN BE MADE QUITE EYE-CATCHING WITH THE ADDITION OF A FEW BEADS.

1 Open a pin and thread beads onto the shank of the pin. Use different coloured beads to make an attractive design. Make several pins in the same way.

2 Thread the pins onto two bits of elastic and you have a superb bracelet. Put the pins alternately the right way up and upside down. This is so they will fit together neatly. Now put the bracelet over your wrist. Very glamorous indeed!

3 Another thing you could do with your bead-covered pins is to thread them onto the shank of another pin. This can then be pinned on your clothing to make an attractive brooch.

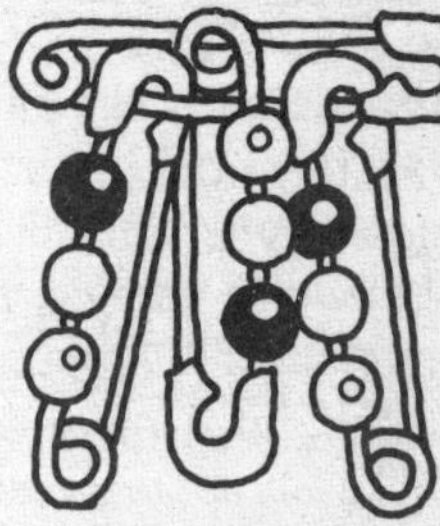

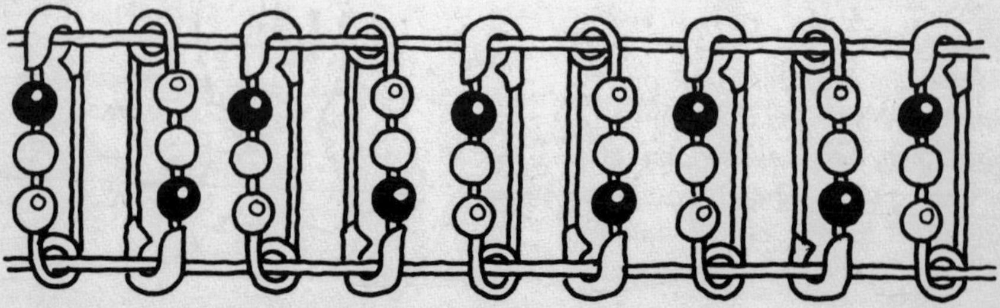

# HOW TO BALANCE A SPOON ON YOUR NOSE

It looks weird. It looks impossible. But it's really quite easy!

1 **T**he secret, if there is one, is to first wipe the top of your nose with a clean, dry cloth. This gets rid of any grease and perspiration.

2 **S**ecretly breathe into the bowl of the spoon to create some moisture, and then place the bowl of the spoon on your nose.

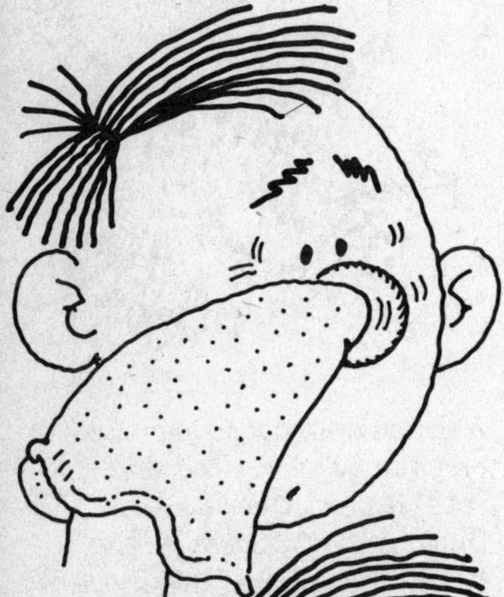

3 **W**ith a bit of luck the spoon will stay in place.

For some reason not everyone can do this. Perhaps there is a special knack to it. Try it and see if it works for you.

# HOW CAN AN OWL TELL YOU WHO LIVES NEARBY?

To discover who lives in the same neighbourhood as an owl, simply find out what the owl ate at a recent meal.

You can get this information from an owl pellet.

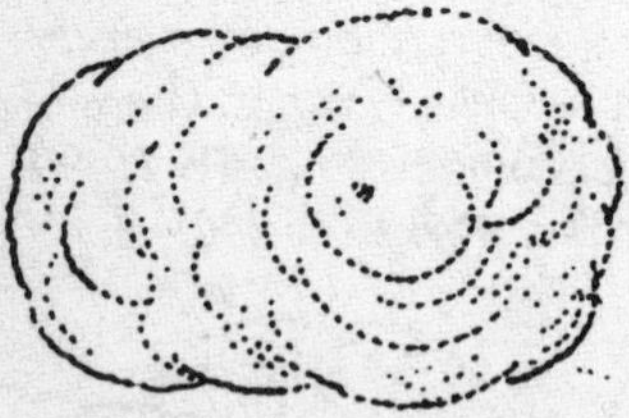

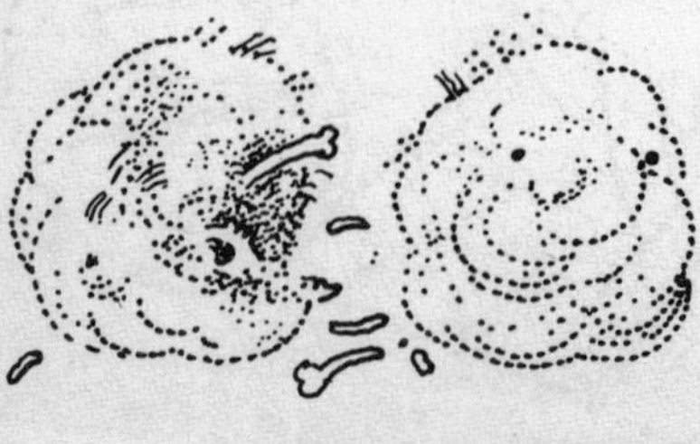

When an owl swoops in on its prey (small mice, voles, and rats) it picks them up whole. But owls can't digest all the bones. To overcome this problem, they regurgitate (bring up) all the indigestible matter in a small pellet, a neat package of bones and fur.

These owl pellets can be found on the ground in areas inhabited by owls. By dissecting the pellet it is possible to see all the bones and work out what animal has been eaten and thus find out who lives nearby.

# HOW CAN YOU BUILD A TANK?

ALL YOU NEED TO BUILD THIS AMAZING MOVING TANK IS A COTTON-REEL, AN ELASTIC BAND, TWO MATCHSTICKS AND A PIECE OF CANDLE.

1 Make a hole in the centre of the candle. Now thread the elastic band through both the cotton-reel and the candle.

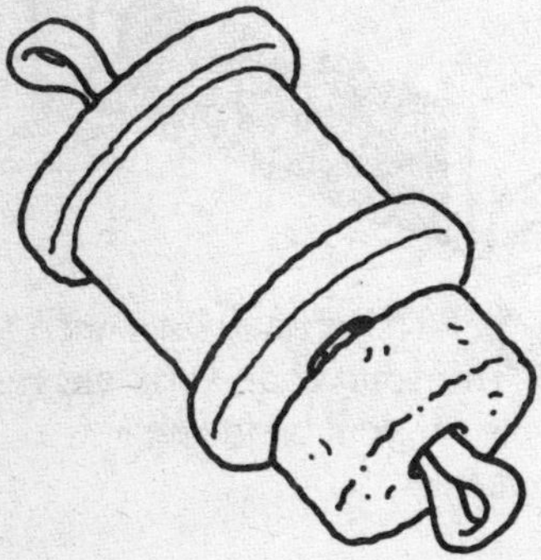

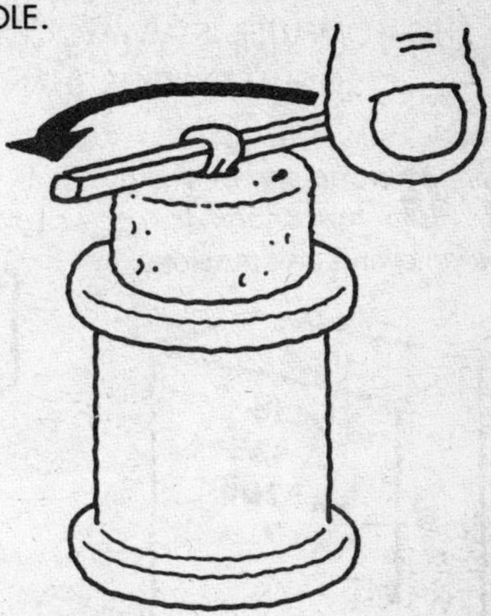

2 Hold the band in place with a long matchstick at the candle end, and a small piece of matchstick at the other end.

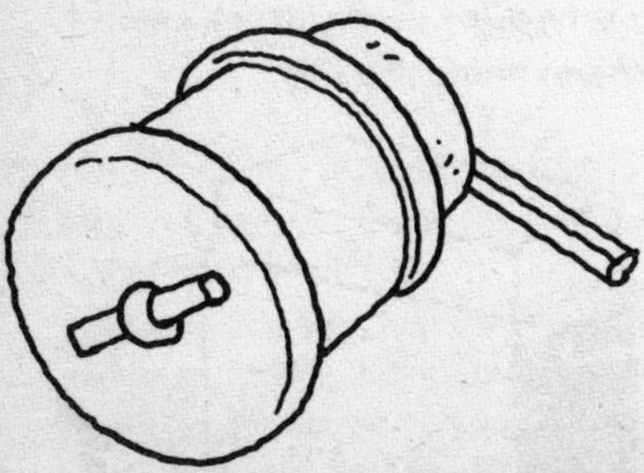

3 Wind up the engine by turning the long match round and round.

4 Place your tank on the floor and off it goes!

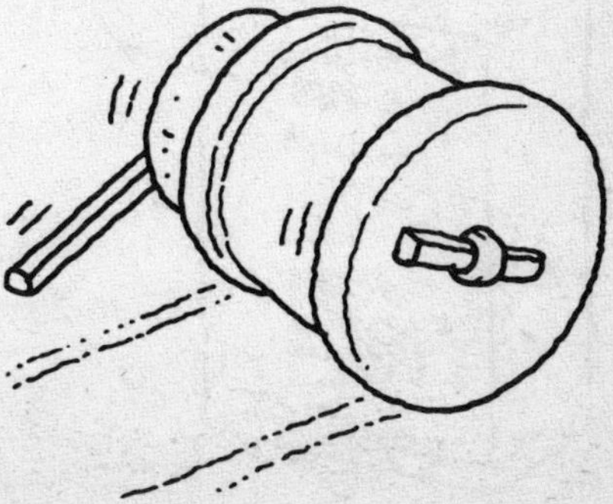

# HOW CAN YOU MAKE A COMPUTER OUT OF A MATCHBOX?

THIS COMPUTER IS ALWAYS CORRECT, AND IT CAN WORK OUT A SUM QUICKER THAN ANY MATHEMATICIAN.

1. On one end of the base of a matchbox drawer write the following calculations.

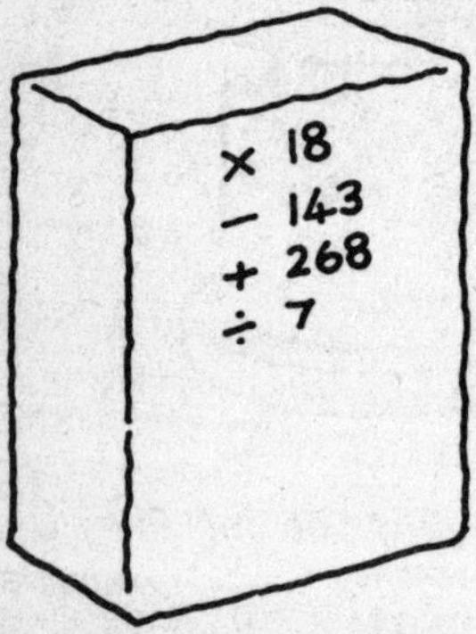


2. At the other end of the drawer write the word 'correct'.

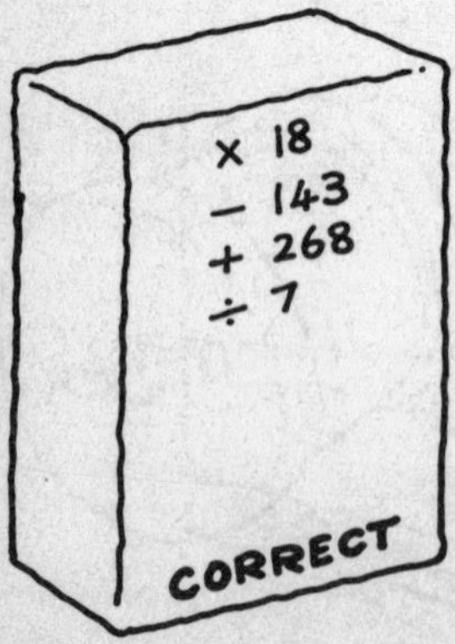


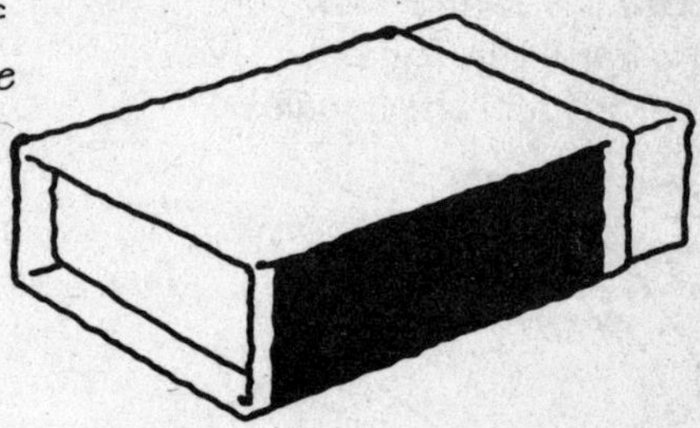

3. Put the drawer back into the matchbox and you are ready to show off your amazing computer.

4. Ask a friend to write down any number. Bring out your incredible, infallible matchbox computer and push out the drawer so that the first calculation (x 18) is visible. Ask your friend to multiply their chosen number by 18.

5 **P**ush up the drawer a little further to show the next calculation (-143) and ask your friend to deduct 143 from the figure they now have.

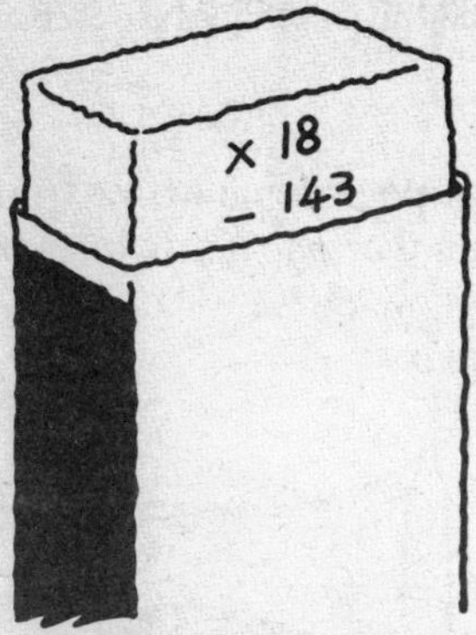


6 **D**o exactly the same with the next two calculations.

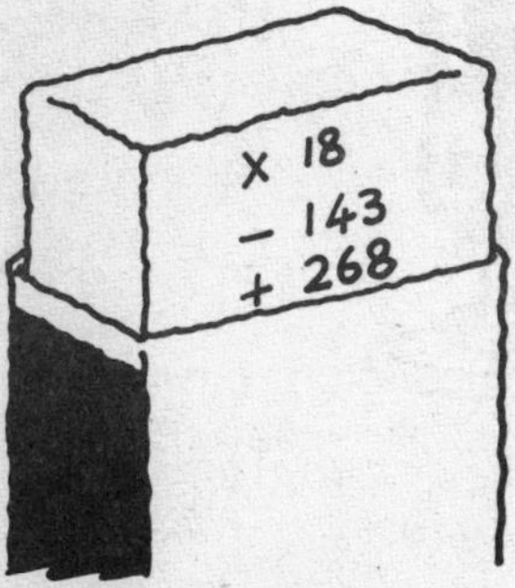


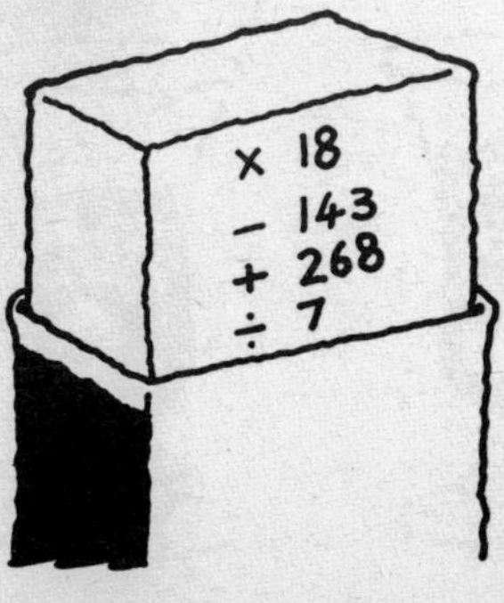


7 **N**ow ask your friend to call out the final answer.

8 **W**hatever it is, you simply push the matchbox drawer out at the other end to show your computer's answer 'correct'. It never fails.

# HOW FULL IS A GLASS?

FOR THIS PROBLEM YOU WILL NEED TO ASK YOUR MUM IF YOU CAN BORROW SEVERAL SHERRY GLASSES, ALL THE SAME SHAPE AND SIZE.

It can be tricky, so you will have to do some advance preparation before showing this to anyone.

1 Fill one of the sherry glasses to the brim with water. We will call this glass **number one**.

2 Now pour some water from number one glass into one o the others, which we will call **number two**.

3 Put varying amounts of water (from a jug or a tap) into the other glasses. You are now ready to fool your friends.

4 Show your pal glass one and all the other glasses. Challenge him or her to say which glass should be used to fill glass one to the brim.

Because sherry glasses are thinner at the bottom than they are at the top your friend will find this almost impossible to do.

5 Provided you remember which glass was your number two glass you can show them which one is the right one.

Although this trick doesn't sound very difficult, your friends will be baffled and you will amaze them with your skill.

# HOW CAN YOU TURN A MATCHBOX INTO A TOP?

YOU WOULD THINK THAT A MATCHBOX WAS COMPLETELY THE WRONG SHAPE TO MAKE A TOP FROM. HOWEVER, IT CAN BE DONE.

1 Remove the drawer from a matchbox and put it to one side. You won't be needing it. Take the matchbox sleeve and flatten it.

2 Now cut it into four equal pieces.

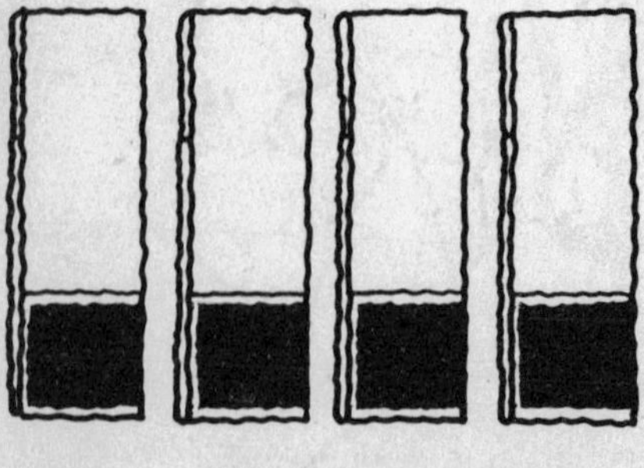

3 Take two pieces and push the non-striking end of one into the striking end of the other.

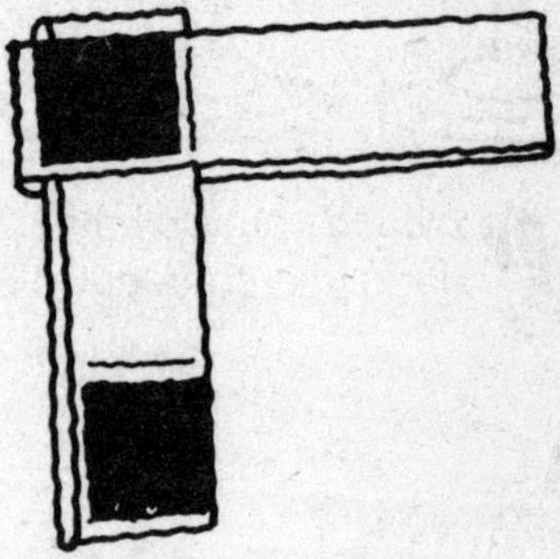

4 Fit the other two pieces together in the same way and then put all four pieces together so they interlock.

5 Push all four pieces into the centre so you have the shape of a square.

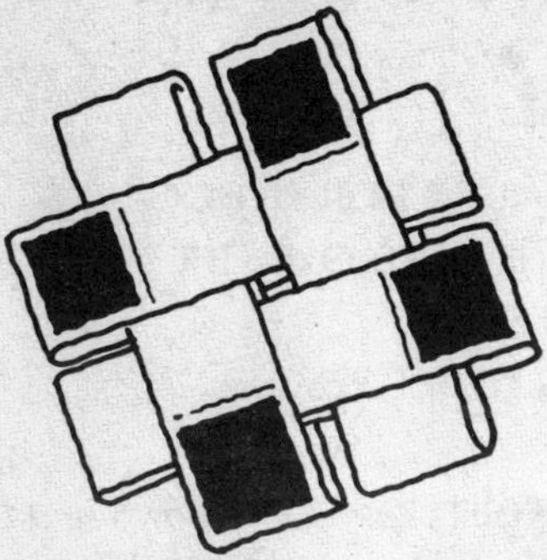

6 Now it gets a bit complicated. Take the opposite corners and push them into the middle.

7 Take a match and push it through the centre of your matchbox shape.

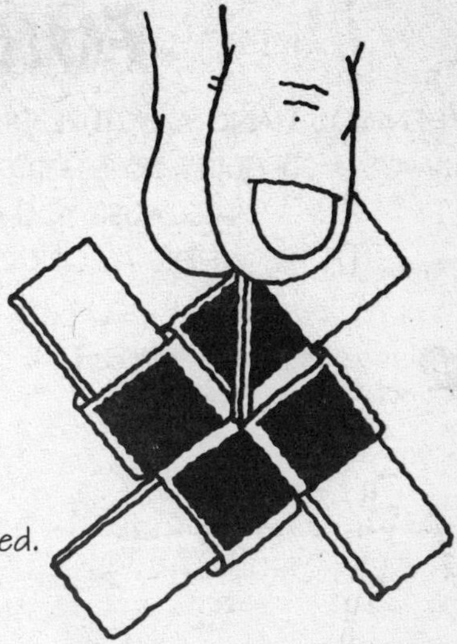

8 Tighten everything up and you have a perfect matchbox top which will spin quite well on the matchstick.

# HOW CAN YOU HANG A PICTURE WITH A FORK?

WHEN YOU HANG A PICTURE ON A NAIL OR PICTURE HOOK IT'S ALWAYS A BIT FIDDLY TRYING TO GET THE CORD OVER THE NAIL BECAUSE YOU CAN'T SEE IT.
THIS IS WHERE A FORK COMES TO THE RESCUE.

1 Place the prongs of the fork over the nail or hook.

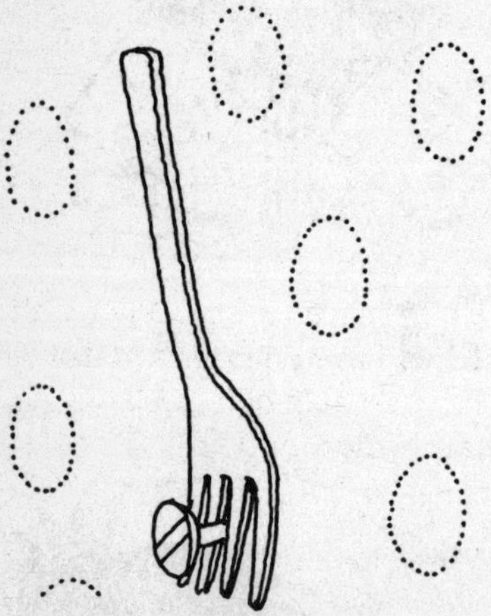

2 Now it is quite an easy matter to thread the cord over the top end of the fork.

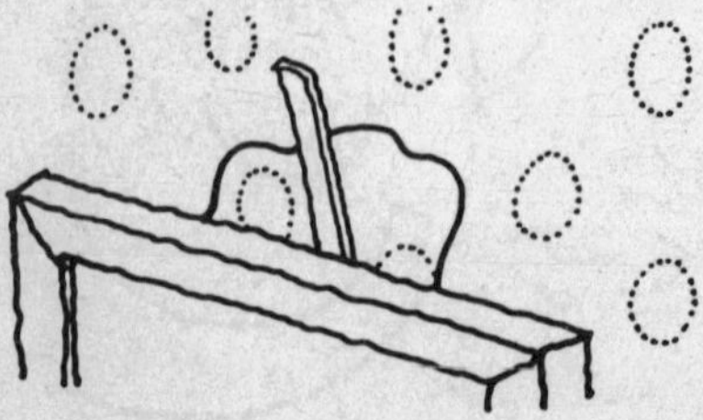

3 Pull the picture down and the cord goes down behind the fork and onto the hook or nail.

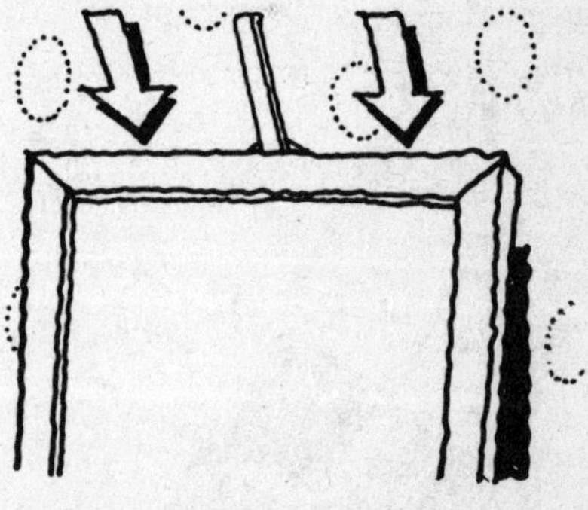

4 Remove the fork and the operation is complete.

# HOW CAN YOU MAKE A MATCHSTICK STAND TO ATTENTION?

EVERYONE WILL THINK THAT YOU ARE USING GLUE WHEN YOU SHOW A MATCHSTICK STANDING TO ATTENTION ON YOUR THUMB. BUT YOU DON'T NEED GLUE. YOU JUST HAVE TO CHEAT A LITTLE.

1 Take a dead matchstick and place it against the joint of your bent thumb. Push it quite hard into the skin (but not so hard that you hurt yourself).

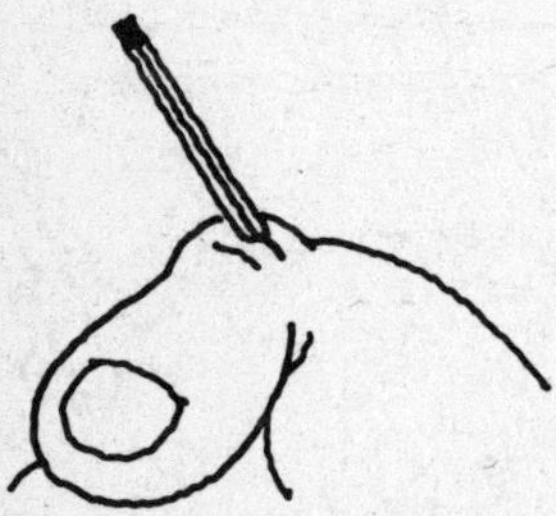

2 Now straighten your thumb and the match will remain standing upright.

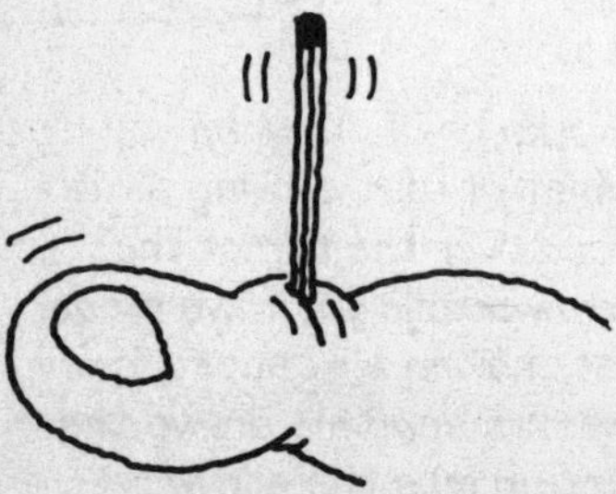

It does this because it is held by the little wrinkles of skin on the top of the thumb joint.

There is no need to tell your friends how you do this. Let them work it out for themselves!

# HOW DO YOU PAINT WITH A STRAW?

TO PAINT WITH A DRINKING STRAW YOU MUST FIRST TURN THE STRAW INTO A PAINT SPRAY.

SOUNDS LIKE A TALL ORDER, DOESN'T IT? BUT IN FACT, IT'S QUITE EASY TO DO.

1 Take an ordinary drinking straw and about a third of the way from one end make a slit three-quarters of the way through it.

2 Bend the straw at this point.

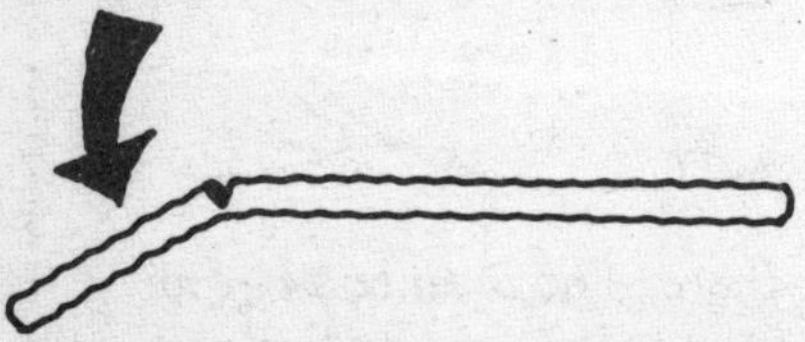

3 Now insert a piece from a small straw into the short end of the first one.

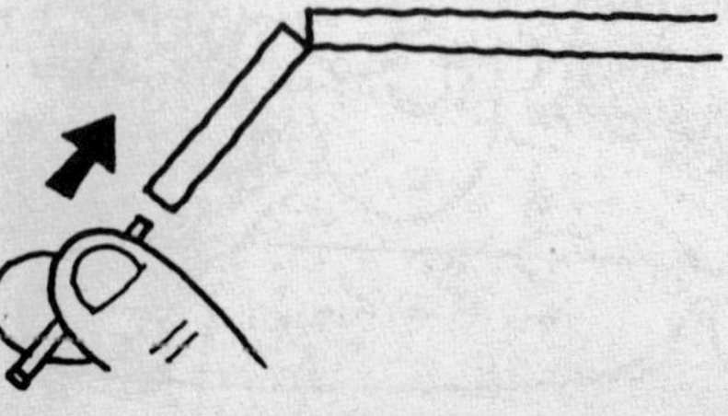

4 Put the short end of the straw into a bottle of paint and blow through the other end. You will produce a fine spray of paint. Whatever you do, don't suck or you may get a mouthful of paint.

It works because when you blow, a blast of fast-moving air is forced over the top of the narrow nozzle you have made. Fast-moving air causes lower pressure and this draws the paint up into the straw.

**5** **P**ut a cut-out stencil of any shape you like on a sheet of paper and then use your straw- spray to cover it with paint. When you lift the stencil it will leave a clear outline surrounded by paint.

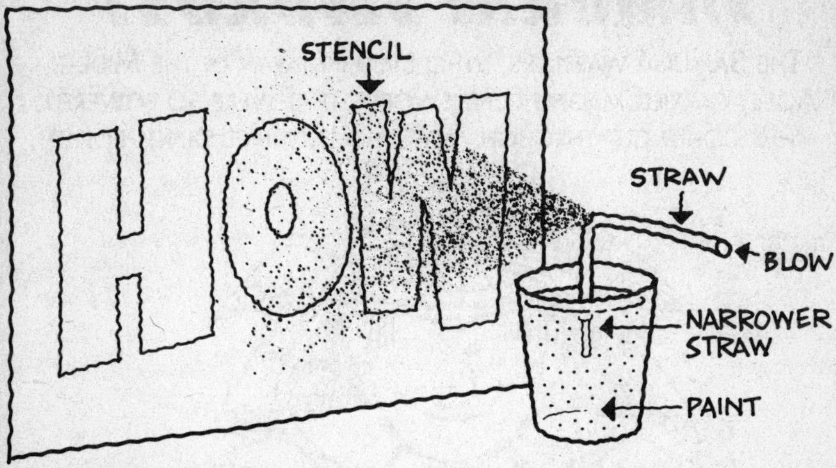

Make several different stencils and use lots of different colours and you will be able to produce a masterpiece.

# HOW DID THEY MAKE SAMURAI SWORDS?

THE SAMURAI WARRIORS, WHO LIVED IN JAPAN IN THE MIDDLE AGES, CARRIED MAGNIFICENT SWORDS THAT WERE SO POWERFUL THEY COULD CUT THROUGH ANYTHING . . . INCLUDING PEOPLE!

But what made the Samurai sword so strong?

Its secret was in the way it was made. Believe it or not, it was made from over a million layers of metal.

That may sound impossible – you would think it would take many years to make something with a million layers. But the Japanese did it in a special way.

Fold something in half and you get 2 layers. Fold it again and you have 4 layers. The next fold gives 8 layers, the next 16 and the one after that 32. Continue like this and after only ten folds you will have 1,024 layers. After 20 folds there will be 1,048,576 layers!

And that's how the Japanese produced the swords for the Samurai warriors!

# HOW DO YOU WALK WITHOUT LOSING YOUR BALANCE?

WE TAKE THE ACTION OF WALKING SO MUCH FOR GRANTED THAT WE SELDOM THINK ABOUT HOW WE ACTUALLY DO IT.

When you walk you lift up your leg and throw it forward. At this point you have not moved. To actually move, you have to bring the other leg into play. But to do this you must put the first leg down . . . but to put it down you have to lose your balance. You have to fall forward slightly until the foot reaches the ground.

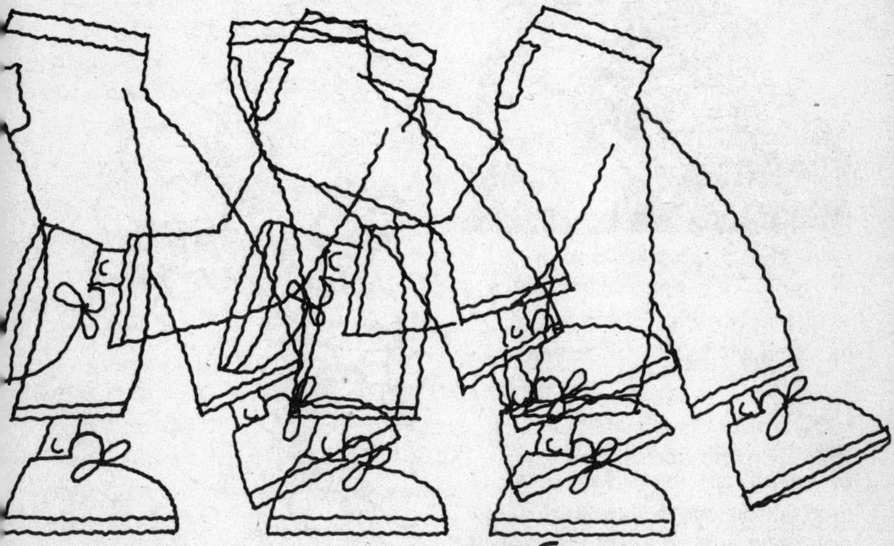

Every step is done in this manner, so when you are walking you are constantly losing and regaining your balance.

# HOW DID THEY STOP SCOTLAND FROM BLOWING UP?

IN 1866, THE SWEDISH CHEMIST ALFRED NOBEL INVENTED DYNAMITE. HE SET UP A FACTORY IN THE WILDS OF SCOTLAND TO PRODUCE THE EXPLOSIVES.

The most explosive and dangerous part of dynamite is nitroglycerine. This must be handled with the utmost care.

One man in the explosive factory had the important job of watching the nitroglycerine mixture to make sure that it did not overheat and explode. But it was such a boring job that it was likely he would nod off to sleep.

The problem was how to keep the man awake and stop the factory, and Scotland, from being blown to pieces.

They found the answer in the dynamite stool. No, it wasn't a stool made of dynamite that exploded when the worker fell asleep. It was a stool with just one leg. If the worker became tired and nodded off to sleep, he would also fall off the stool!

So, it was the dynamite stool which kept him awake, stopped the mixture from boiling over, stopped the factory from exploding and saved Scotland from being blown to smithereens!

# HOW DO YOU MAKE A RUBBER BAND JUMP?

HOW CAN YOU MAKE A RUBBER BAND JUMP FROM TWO OF YOUR FINGERS TO TWO OTHER FINGERS?

It is an amazing feat that will baffle your friends but which is, in fact, quite easy to do.

All you need is a rubber band and a pair of hands.

1. Place the rubber band over the first and second fingers of your left hand.

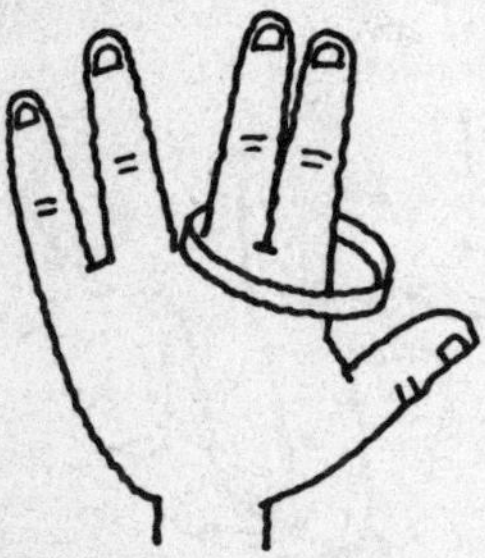

2. With your right hand stretch the band down towards your left palm.

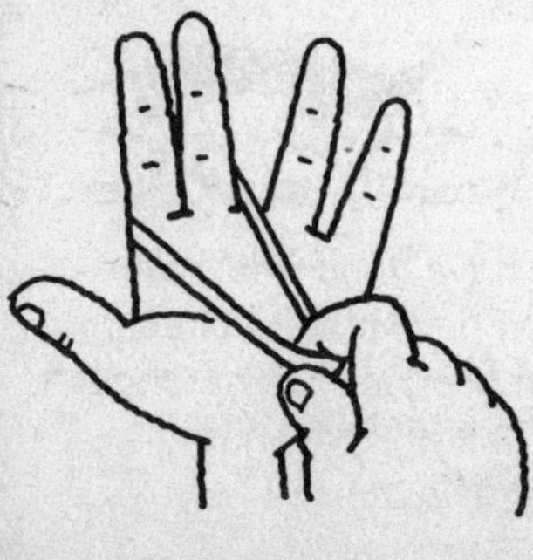

3. You now have to do three actions at the same time. Your right hand has to let go of the band at exactly the same time that your left hand turns over and closes into a fist, making sure that all four fingers of your left hand go into the rubber band.

4. From the front it appears that the band is still over your first two fingers. Now all you have to do is open your hand and the band will jump off your first two fingers and over the third and fourth fingers.

It looks as if the band has jumped through your fingers by magic.

# HOW CAN YOU WIN SOME MONEY WITH SOME MONEY?

**1** Borrow two 10p coins from your friends. Place the two coins on a table so that they touch each other.

**2** Now bring out a 2p coin. Bet that you can place the 2p between the two 10ps without moving one 10p and without touching the other.

If your friends take up your challenge, ask them if they are prepared to bet their 10ps that you can't do it.

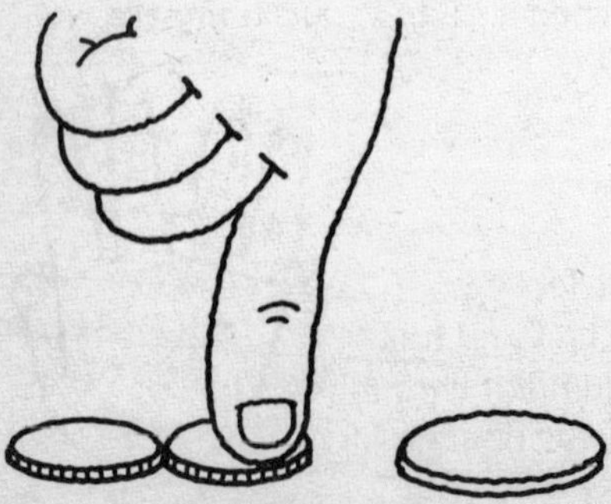

**3** To win the bet all you have to do it place your finger on one of the 10p coins. Now propel the 2p coin across the table so it hits the 10p held by your finger.

The momentum of the blow will pass through the 10p you are touching and the other 10p will be knocked away.

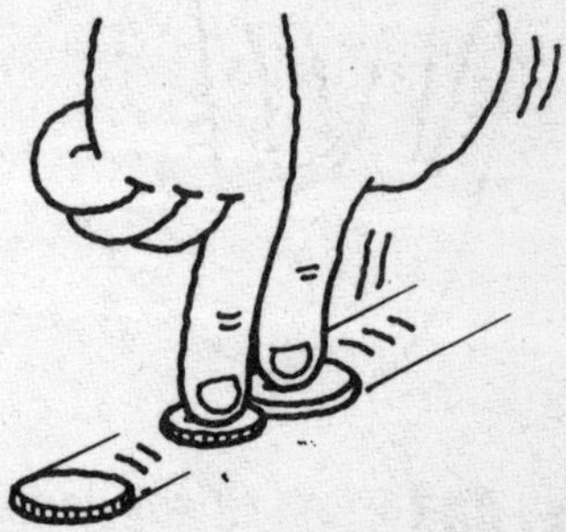

**4** You can now move the 2p coin around to fill the gap.

So, you have done what you said. You have placed the 2p between the two 10ps without moving one and without touching the other.

# HOW TO TELL A SLOW-WORM FROM A SNAKE

THE MAIN DIFFERENCE IS THAT THE SLOW-WORM IS NOT A SNAKE BUT A LEGLESS LIZARD.

Although they are completely different animals their skeletons are almost identical.

To tell the difference you need to take a close look. Snakes' eyes have no eyelids so they stare continually without blinking. A slow-worm, on the other hand, does have eyelids and blinks just as we do.

Look at a snake's mouth and it appears to be smiling. This is because snakes can dislocate (unhinge) their jaws in order to swallow large prey. However, the jaw bone of a slow-worm is constructed in a way very similar to that of a human.

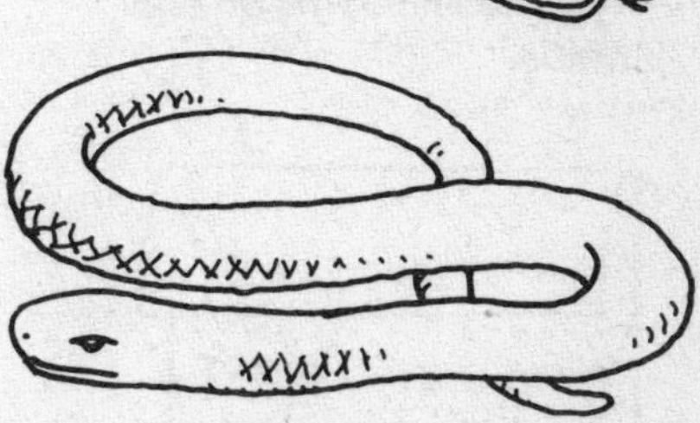

Another distinct feature of snakes is that they have forked tongues which dart in and out very quickly. The slow-worm's tongue is much slower in action.

One other thing to remember – if you see something two metres long slithering towards you, it is certainly not a slow-worm. Time for you to make a hasty exit!

# HOW CAN YOU MAKE A KIMONO?

A KIMONO IS AN ELEGANT ROBE WORN BY THE JAPANESE.

**YOU WILL NEED:** some material, a pair of scissors, a needle and some thread.

1. Fold the material a quarter of the way down from the top.

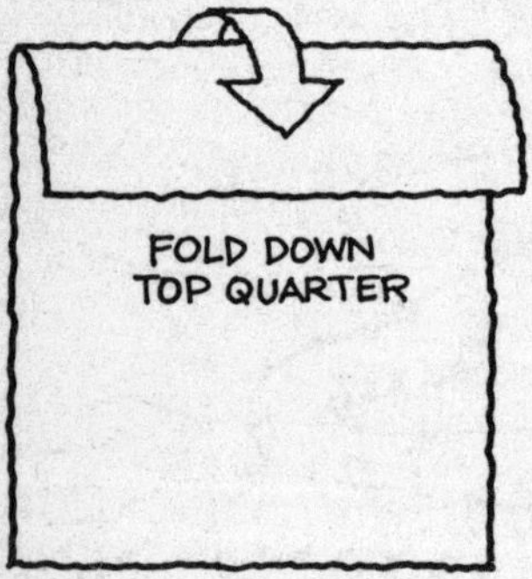


2. Next, cut in approximately a quarter of the way along and then do the same on the other side.

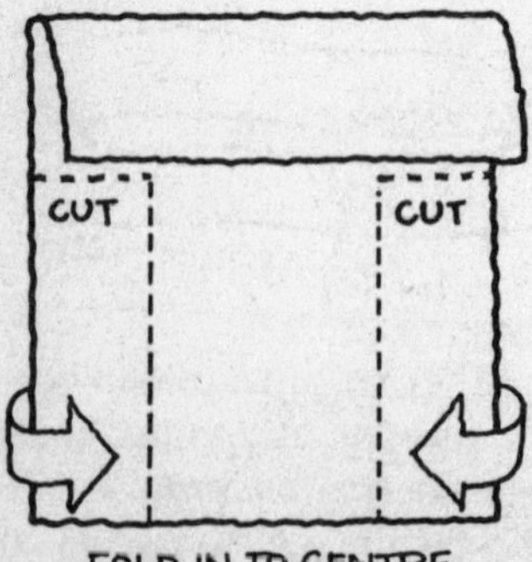


3. Then, make one of the sleeves by cutting through both pieces of cloth half way up. Do the same on the other side to form the other sleeve.

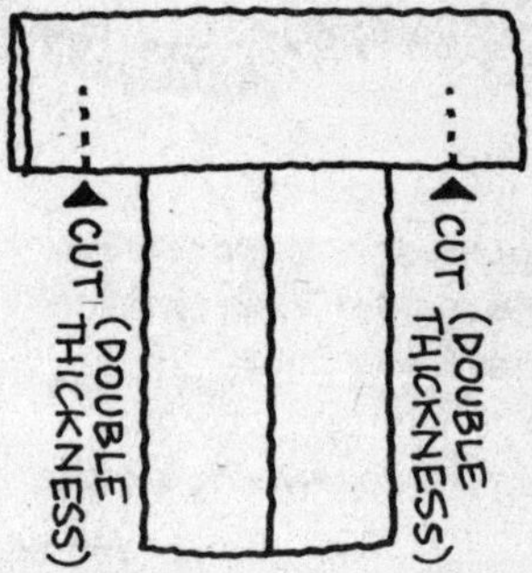


4. Now cut up the centre of the front of the material to the top.

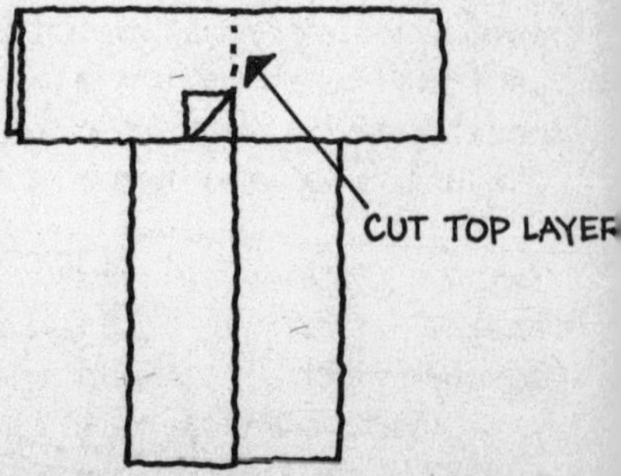

5 Sew along the base of both sleeves. Then sew the top centre portions to the lower centre portions.

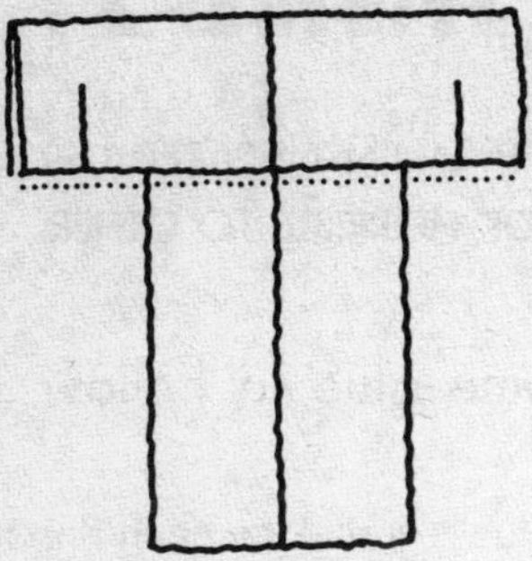

SEW ALONG DOTTED SECTIONS

You now have a kimono that you can wear around the house. Very comfortable, very elegant and very simple to make.

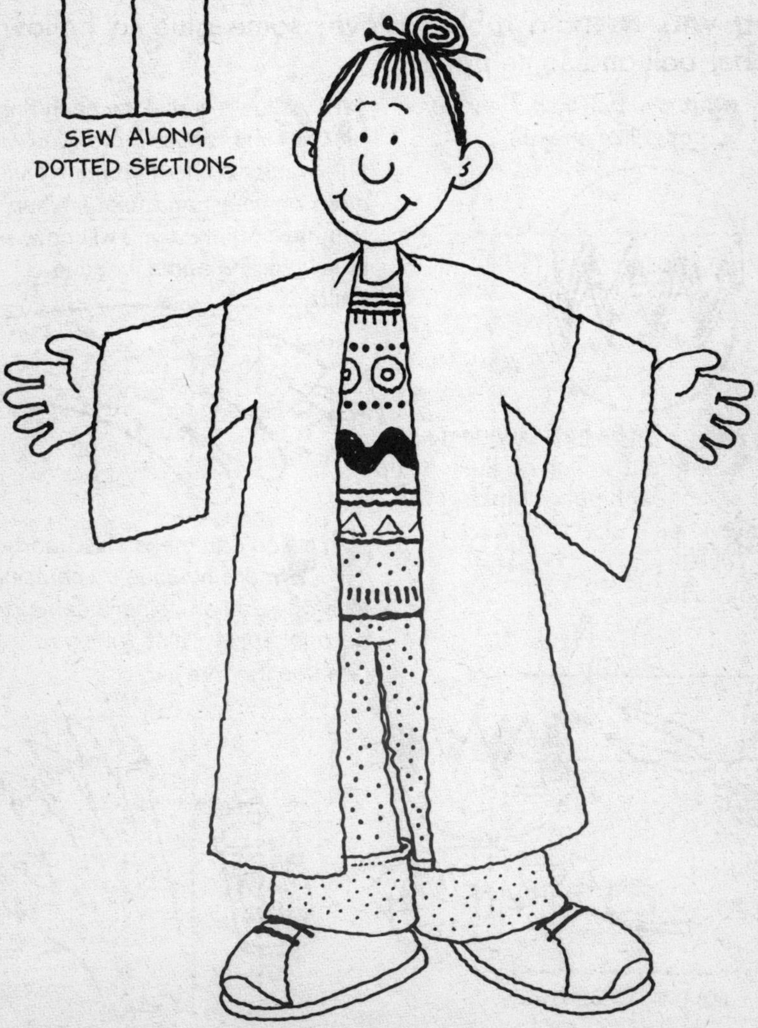

# HOW CAN YOU HORRIFY YOUR HANDS?

IT'S DIFFICULT TO HORRIFY YOUR HANDS. THEY AREN'T SCARED OF ANYTHING. BUT TO MAKE YOUR HANDS LOOK HORRIBLE TO OTHER PEOPLE IS QUITE EASY.

**YOU WILL NEED:** a rubber glove, some glue, a hollow rubber ball and some paints.

1 Cut the ball into a series of petal-like shapes.

2 Cut off the individual petals and put a blob of glue on the wide end of each petal. Make sure you use a glue that works with rubber and not one that dissolves it.

3 Glue a 'petal' to each finger of the rubber glove (you will find this easier to do if you put the glove on your hand first). When you have finished you will have a hand bearing some hideous nails.

4 You can make this hand even more hideous by painting it in lots of ghoulish colours using an aerosol spray paint (one you can use indoors).

# HOW TO MAKE STUFF

WHAT IS STUFF? WELL . . . STUFF IS . . . STUFF. THERE IS NO OTHER WORD FOR IT. BUT IT'S FUN AND EASY TO MAKE.

Tip a tin of cornflour into a large bowl and then add water, a little at a time, until you get a dough-like consistency. This is stuff.

Grab a handful of the stuff. You will find that it goes solid.

Hold your hand over the bowl, and let the stuff drip slowly from your fingers. Give it a shock, by banging it hard, and it will turn solid. Leave it alone and it will become liquid again.

# HOW DO YOU GET OUT OF ROPE HANDCUFFS?

For this amazing trick you will need two pieces of soft rope or string, each about a metre long, and two willing friends.

1. Tie the end of one rope around a friend's wrist, and the other end around the other wrist.

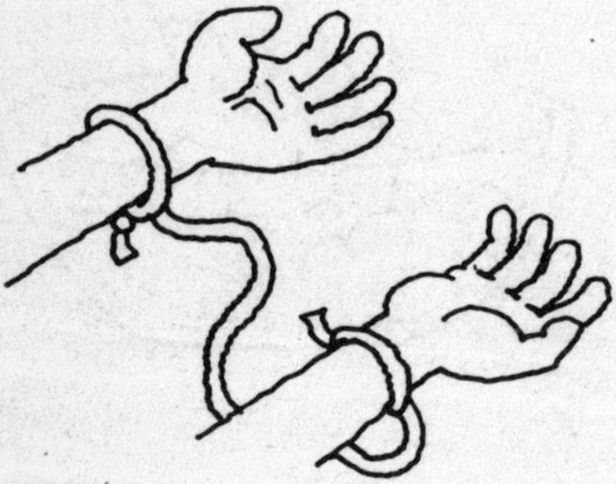

2. Tie another friend's wrists in the same way, but this time link the rope through the first rope, as shown, before tying the wrists.

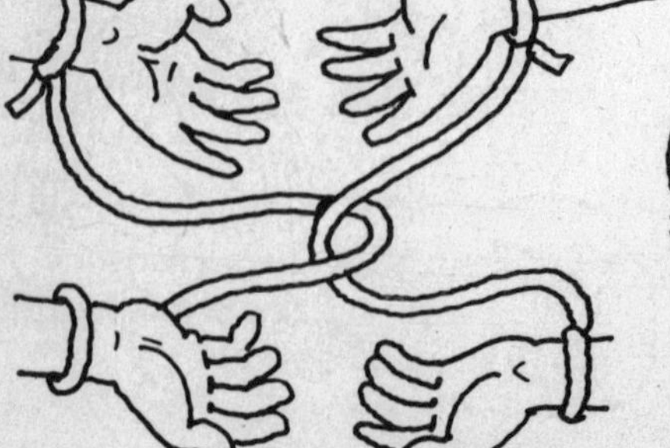

3. Now challenge your friends to separate themselves without cutting or untying the ropes and without wriggling their wrists free. Sit back and enjoy their frustration as they try to get out of their predicament. Eventually they'll give up and you'll have to show them how it's done.

4 Take a loop from the centre of the rope. Push the loop under the rope tying one of the wrists of the other person.

5 Next pass the loop of rope over the hand and the two ropes are now separated.

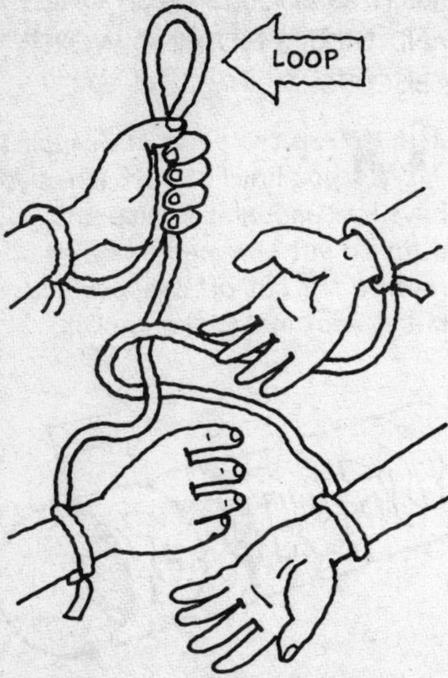


PUSH LOOP THROUGH OTHER PERSON'S WRIST FASTENING

PASS LOOP OVER HAND

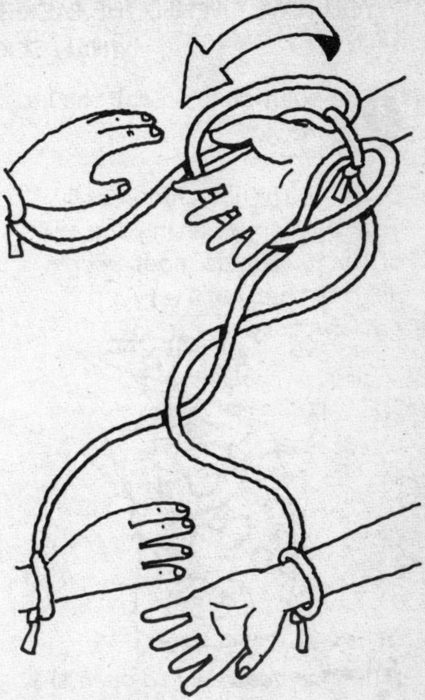

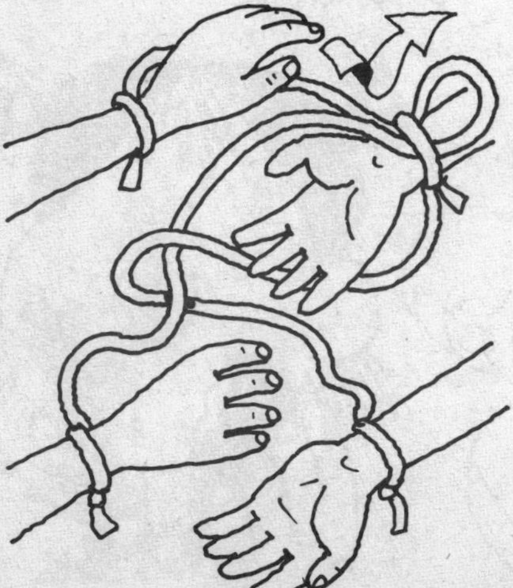

# WARNING

**Remember – never put a rope around your own or anyone else's neck, as it can be dangerous.**

# HOW CAN YOU KEEP BISCUITS FRESH?

IT CAN SOMETIMES BE A PROBLEM KEEPING BISCUITS FRESH ONCE YOU HAVE OPENED THE PACKET – AND THERE'S NOTHING WORSE THAN SOGGY BISCUITS.

One solution is to eat the lot in one go.

But if you're not that greedy, you could try twisting the end of the packet as most people do. But that isn't very satisfactory.

1 The best way to open the packet is by cutting through it with a knife a short distance from one end.

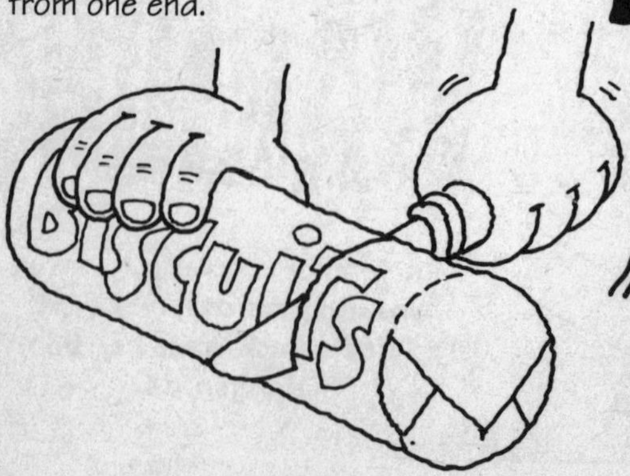

2 Keep the piece of wrapping you have cut off. When you have had enough biscuits and want to put the rest away, reverse the cut off wrapper and put it back inside the packet.

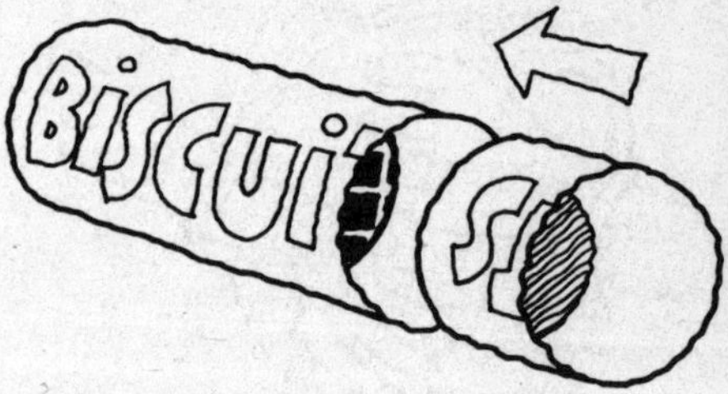

And that is how to keep your biscuits fresh. No more soggy biscuits for you.

# HOW DOES POPCORN POP?

POPCORN IS SIMPLY COOKED DRIED KERNELS OF CORN FROM CORN ON THE COB (OR MAIZE).

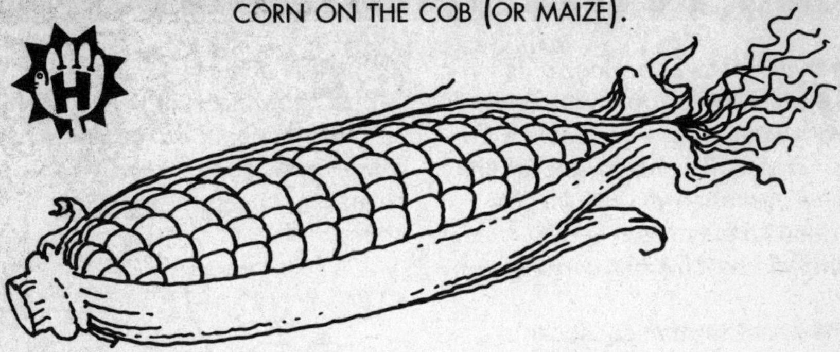

To make it pop it has to be put in a saucepan with a small amount of hot oil, or butter. Within seconds the corn 'pops' and you have popcorn. If you try making it yourself, be careful of the hot oil and make sure that you put a lid on the pan or the room will be showered in popcorn.

You may have made popcorn before but have you ever wondered why it pops?

The outer skin of the kernel is quite tough, but inside it is full of pulp. There is a lot of moisture in the pulp, when the moisture gets hot it gives off steam and pressure is built up inside the kernel. Eventually, the pressure gets so great that the outer skin is unable to hold it. The whole thing explodes, turning the kernel of corn completely inside out, and you have popcorn. Delicious!

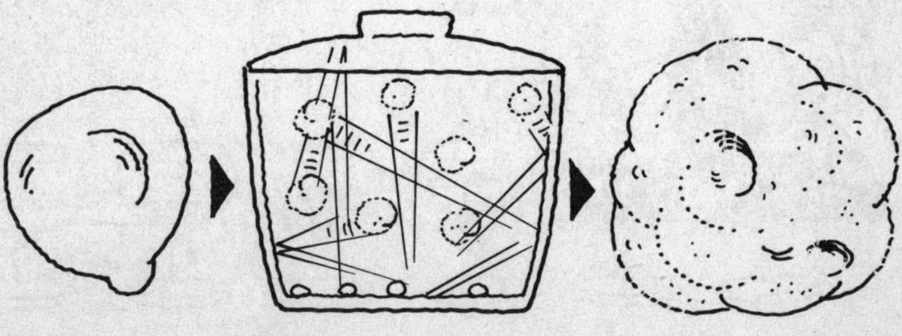

# HOW TO PLAY THE HYDRO DACTYLLO PSYCHIC HARMONICA

Hydro means 'having to do with water'. Dactyllo comes from 'dactyllus' – the Latin word for 'finger'. Psychic means 'of the mind', because you need a few brains to play the *hydro dactyllo psychic harmonica.*

The word 'harmonica' doesn't mean a mouth-organ as you might expect, but means 'pleasant music'. In the past it was used to describe a musical glass. And that is what a hydro dactyllo psychic harmonica is – 'a musical glass'.

1. Put some water on your forefinger and then rub it around the rim of a wine glass. With practice you should be able to make a tuneful 'ringing' sound.

2. You can change the pitch of this sound by putting water in the glass.

3. Fill several glasses with different levels of water and you can play a tune.

# HOW TO BALANCE A FORK, A SPOON AND A MATCHSTICK ON A PIN

THIS SOUNDS IMPOSSIBLE AND YOUR FRIENDS WILL NOT BELIEVE YOU CAN DO IT. BUT YOU CAN!

**YOU WILL NEED:** a spoon, a fork, a matchstick, a pin, a cork and its bottle.

1 **F**irst push the bowl of the spoon into the prongs of the fork so they hold together. Don't use your best cutlery for this, as it might get scratched.

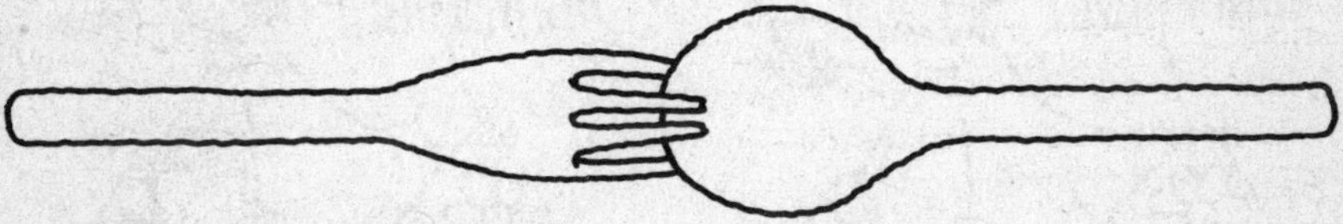

2 **P**ush the match into the middle of the fork prongs.

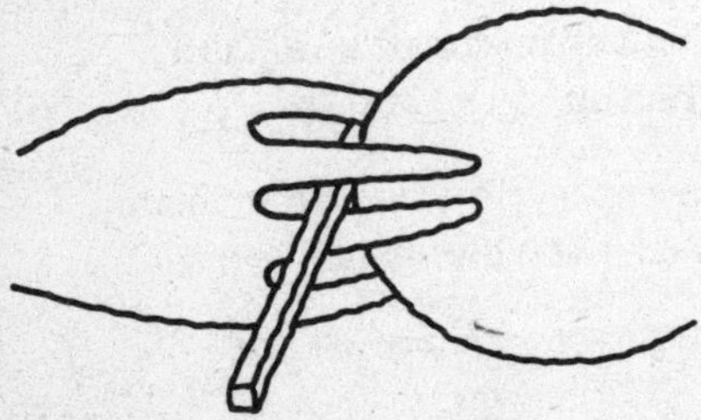

3 **P**ush the cork into the top of the bottle and push the pin into the cork.

4 **W**ith a steady hand and a little patience, carefully balance the match on the pin.

You can even make the fork and spoon spin if you push them very gently and the balance is absolutely correct.

# HOW CAN YOU PLAY A VACUUM CLEANER?

IF YOU PLACE AN EMPTY BOTTLE NEAR YOUR LIPS AND BLOW ACROSS THE TOP OF IT, YOU'LL PRODUCE A HUMMING SOUND.

This is because the air vibrating across the top of the bottle also makes the bottle vibrate and this vibration is what you hear.

If you put water in the bottle you will get a different sound.

You can get the same effect by placing the nozzle of a vacuum cleaner, with a reverse thrust, near the top of the bottle.

Put several bottles in a row with different levels of water in them. Switch on your vacuum cleaner and see if you can play a tune.

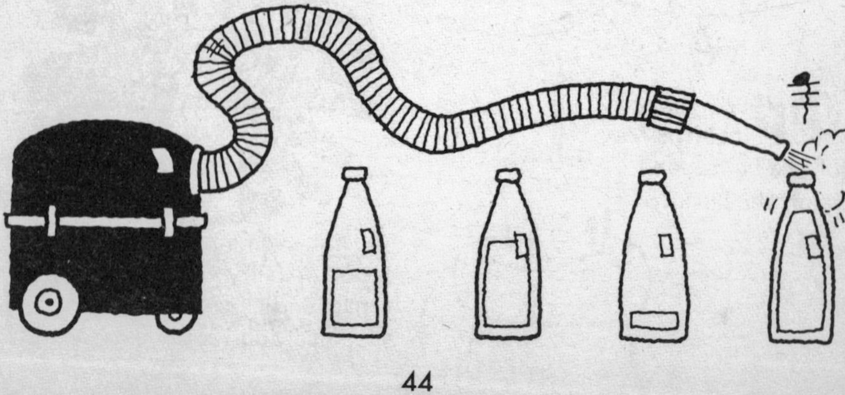

# HOW CAN PASTA BE BEAUTIFUL?

PASTA IS NOT ONLY GREAT TO EAT, IT CAN ALSO MAKE GREAT JEWELLERY.

1 Paint pasta (any sort that has a hole in it) in lots of different colours. You will find that nail varnish is one of the best 'paints' to use because it dries hard and gives a lovely shine.

Some pasta is already coloured, so it doesn't need to be painted.

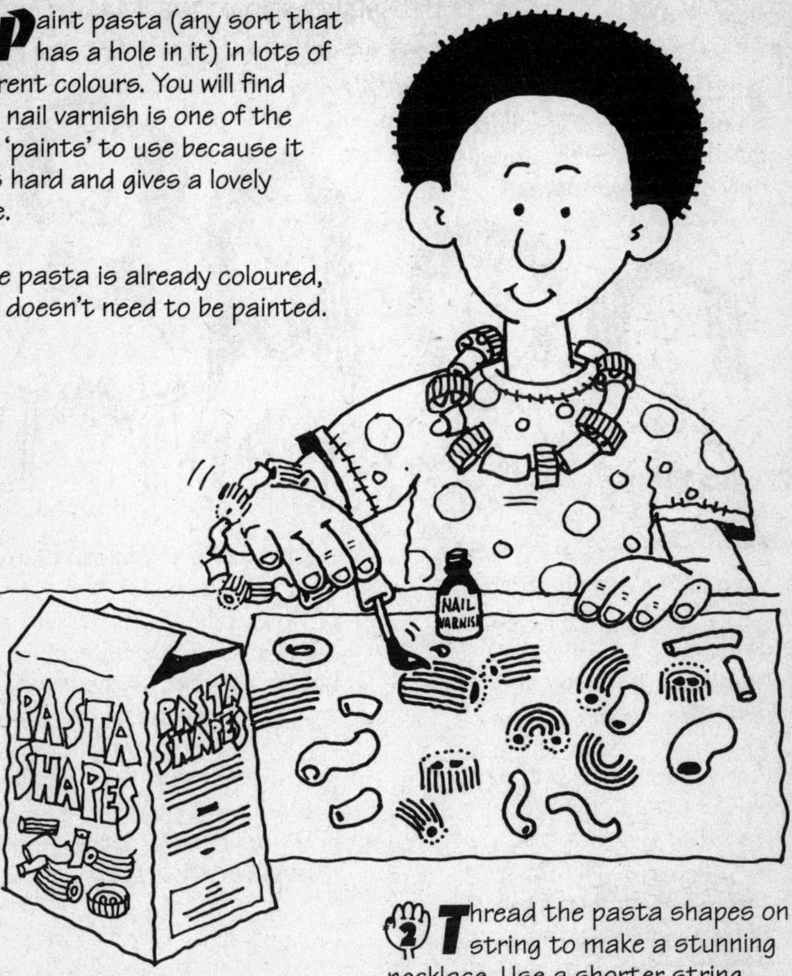


2 Thread the pasta shapes on string to make a stunning necklace. Use a shorter string to make an attractive bracelet. You can also make a pasta tiara in the same way.

# HOW CAN YOU KNOW THE NAMES OF EVERYBODY IN A COUNTRY?

YOU CAN IF YOU GO TO BALI, AN ISLAND IN THE INDIAN OCEAN EAST OF JAVA.

In Bali they have a most unusual custom – all the children born there are given only one of four names.

The first born is always called Wayan. The second is always called Made (pronounced Madday). The third is always called Nyoman, and the fourth is always Ketut.

If the parents have any more children the names are repeated. The fifth child is Wayan, the sixth Made, the seventh Nyoman, the eighth Ketut, the ninth Wayan, and so on, and so on. It doesn't matter whether the child is a boy or a girl, the sequence is always followed.

So, in theory, if you stand in a street in Denpasar, the capital of Bali, and call out 'Wayan' a quarter of the population should respond. Call out 'Made' and another quarter should respond. Call 'Nyoman' and a quarter of the people will think you are calling them. And call out 'Ketut' and another quarter should acknowledge your call.

Call out all four names and presumably everyone in Bali will answer!

# HOW CAN YOU TRICK A FRIEND INTO SOAKING THEMSELVES?

THIS IS A GREAT WAY OF SOAKING UNSUSPECTING FRIENDS.

1 **F**ill a plastic bottle with water and tighten the lid.

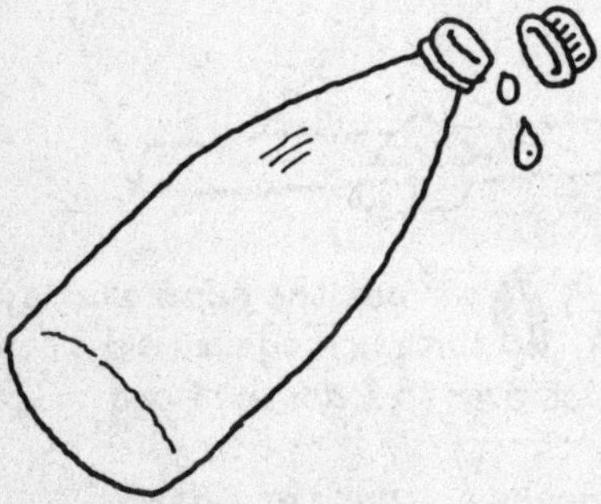

2 **M**ake some small pinholes near the bottom of the bottle. The water won't come out provided that the lid is on tight.

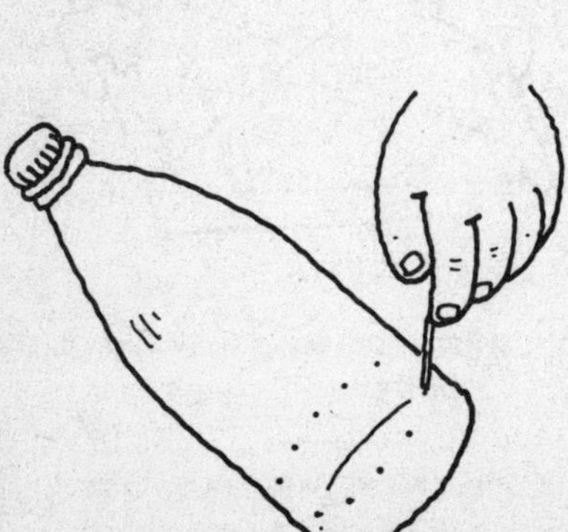

3 **O**ffer a friend a drink from the bottle, and pass it to him or her with the lid still on tight.

4 **W**hen he or she removes the lid, the liquid will pour out through the holes and he or she will get a soaking.

# HOW CAN YOU MAKE A PIECE OF PAPER SPIN?

For this you need a sheet of thin paper – the paper used for airmail letters is ideal.

1 **P**lace the paper down on a flat surface. Fold one corner across to make a diagonal crease.

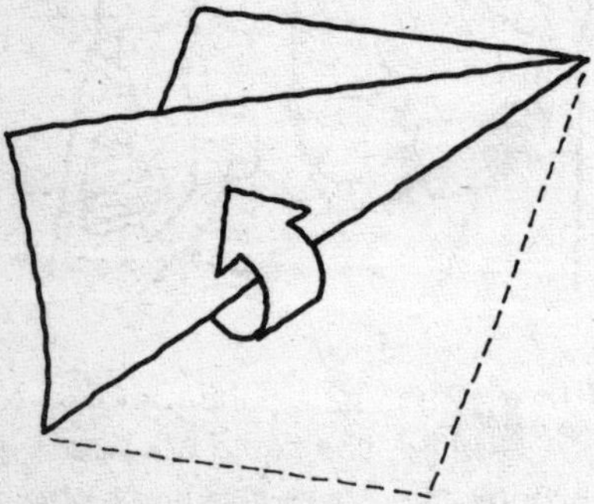

2 **T**urn the paper around and do the same for another diagonal.

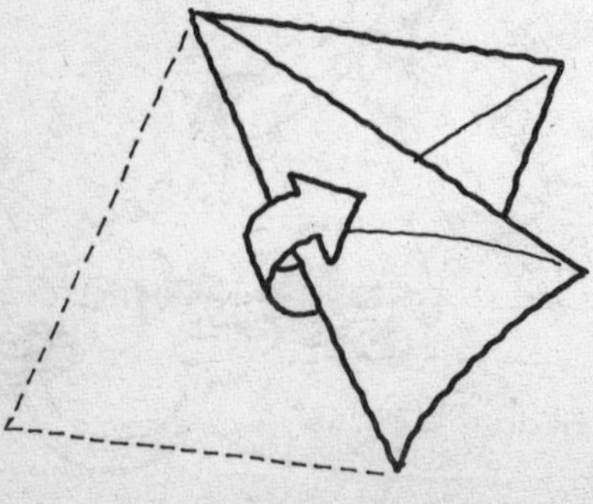

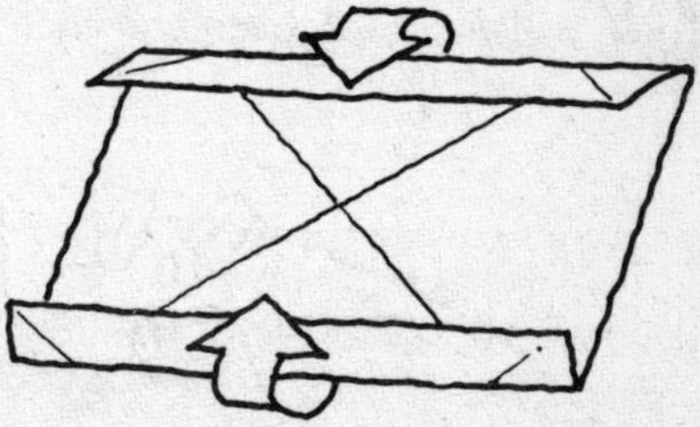

3 **O**pen out the paper and lay it flat once again. Fold all the sides over to a depth of one centimetre. Make strong creases so that the sides stand up.

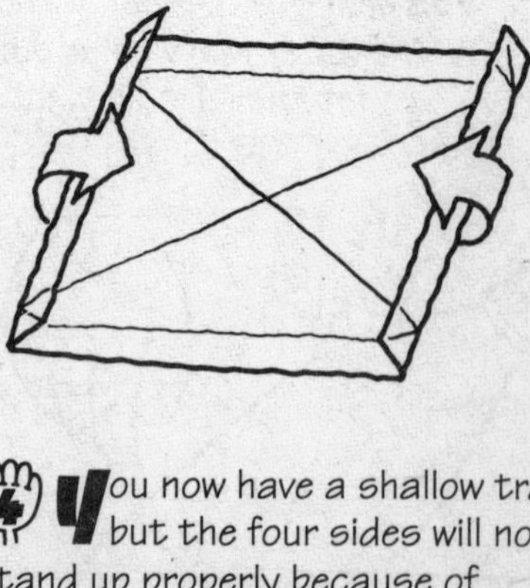

4 **Y**ou now have a shallow tray but the four sides will not stand up properly because of the corners sticking out. Give them a squeeze to help hold everything together.

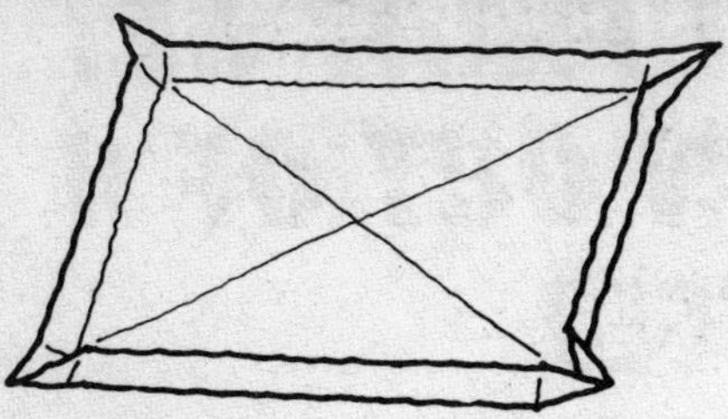

5 Place the paper (with the tray facing outwards) on the forefinger of your right hand. Use the fingers of the left hand inside the tray to keep it in position. Hold your arms out as straight as possible. Now turn around quickly and let go with your left hand. With a bit of luck the paper will spin on the tip of your forefinger.

6 It takes a bit of practice, but eventually you should become so expert that you can keep the paper spinning for quite a long time.

# HOW CAN A FRUIT GET YOU THROWN OUT OF A HOTEL?

The durian tree grows in south-east Asia. It has oblong-shaped leaves, yellowy-green flowers, and bears a large, oval fruit that is covered with wicked-looking spines.

The flesh of the durian fruit is a creamy pulp which has a sweet taste, similar to strawberries. Unfortunately the durian smells really nasty – something like a mouldy conker!

The durian is one of the world's most expensive fruits, costing some £200 a kilo. It is considered a great luxury. Tigers certainly appreciate it – it's the only fruit they eat. Orangutans like it too!

Eating a durian has been described as eating the most delicious strawberry mousse in the smelliest public toilet.

Because of its foul smell it is banned by most Far Eastern hotels. Take one into a hotel and you are likely to get thrown out along with your durian.

# HOW MANY TIMES CAN YOU FOLD A PIECE OF PAPER IN HALF?

How many do you think? Five? Ten? Thirty?

Try it and see. You'll find that you can't do it more than about nine times.

Try it with a larger sheet of paper if you like and see if that makes any difference.

Well, it doesn't! You can still do only about nine folds.

The reason for this is that you are doubling up the number of layers of paper each time you make a fold.

On the first fold you will have two layers of paper. The second fold produces four layers. Third gets 8, 4th equals 16, 5th equals 32, 6th equals 64, 7th makes 128, 8th is 256, 9th makes 512 layers, and if you ever did make that tenth fold you would have an incredible 1024 layers of paper.

# HOW DID CAPTAIN COOK GET HIS MEN TO EAT THEIR CABBAGE?

TWO HUNDRED AND FIFTY YEARS AGO, WHEN CAPTAIN COOK WAS EMBARKING ON HIS EPIC JOURNEYS OF EXPLORATION AND ADVENTURE, SAILORS WERE PRONE TO A DISEASE CALLED SCURVY.

Scurvy was a terrible disease. The victim first developed bruises and a skin rash. Then the gums would become sore and eventually the teeth would fall out. This was followed by internal bleeding and in many cases people eventually died of the disease.

Although Captain Cook did not know this at the time, scurvy is caused by a lack of vegetables and fresh fruit in the diet.

One day, whilst sailing the seven seas, he met the crew of a German ship. He noticed that the German seamen looked incredibly fit and healthy. When asked for the secret of this good health the German captain said it was all due to sauerkraut.

Sauerkaut means 'sour vegetable'. The basic ingredients are chopped cabbage pickled in vinegar.

Captain Cook immediately had some made for his men. He put it in a large barrel bearing a label 'Sauerkraut – it's very good for you'.

But his men thought it was disgusting and refused to eat it.

Cook knew it was good for the men but didn't know how to get them to eat it. After much thought, he came up with a brilliant flash of inspiration. He changed the label on the barrel.

It now read 'For officers only'. Seeing this the men thought that it must be good and ate it. That is how Captain Cook got his men to eat their cabbage and helped to prevent scurvy breaking out on his ships!

# HOW DO MILKMEN PERFORM MAGIC?

MANY MILKMEN USE A SPECIAL WALLET THAT TRAPS MONEY INSIDE IT UNDER TWO STRIPS OF TAPE. WHY NOT MAKE ONE FOR YOURSELF!

1 You will need two pieces of card. Each piece should be slightly larger than a £10 note. Lay the two cards side by side.

2 Lay two bits of tape or ribbon (12 cms long) parallel to each other on the left-hand piece of card and glue the ends underneath the right-hand card.

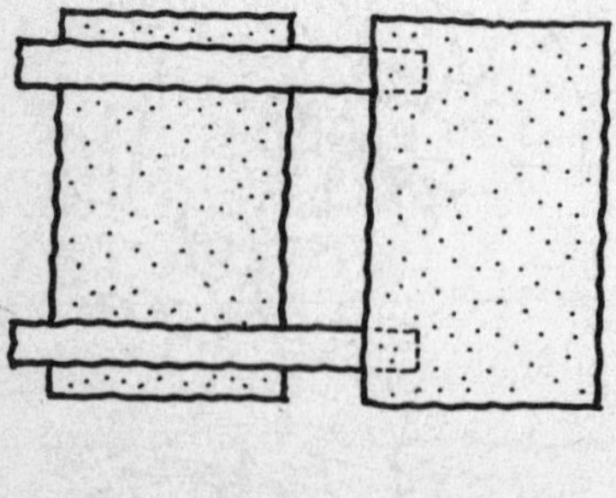

3 Position another two bits of tape, of the same length as the first two, in a cross formation on top of the right-hand piece of card and then stick the ends underneath the other card. Fold over the loose ends of tape and glue them to the reverse side of each card.

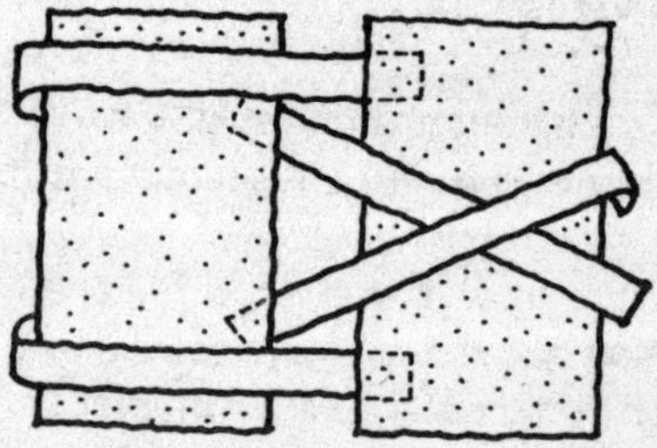

4 Place a £5 note on the left-hand side of the wallet. Close up the wallet by folding the right side over onto the left.

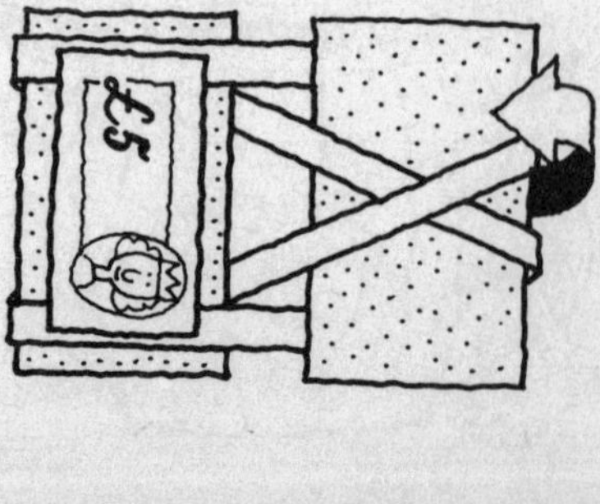

5 Open the wallet again – but this time open the right edge. Your £5 note should now be under the crossed tapes.

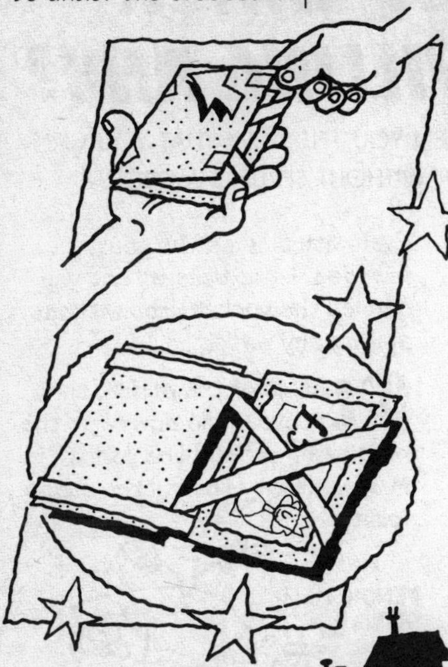

6 Close the wallet again by bringing the right side over onto the left. Now open the right side again and the note is now secure under the parallel tapes.

It must be magic!

# HOW CAN YOU DROP A BUCKET OF WATER WITHOUT SPILLING ANY?

NO-ONE WILL BELIEVE YOU WHEN YOU TELL THEM THAT YOU CAN DROP A BUCKET OF WATER WITHOUT SPILLING A DROP.

1 First you need a little advance preparation. Tie one end of a metre length of string to the handle of a small bucket. Tie the other end of the string to a bunch of keys.

2 Pour some water into the bucket. Hold a pencil in your hand and place the string over the pencil. Pull on the keys until the bucket is pulled right up to the pencil.

Even with this set up your friends will not believe that you can let the bucket drop without spilling any water.

3 Let go of the string, the bucket falls down but the keys swing around the pencil and eventually the bucket stops falling.

Much to everyone's surprise not a drop of water will have been spilt!

# HOW STRONG IS A STRAW?

AMAZINGLY A DRINKING STRAW IS STRONG ENOUGH TO CUT STRAIGHT THROUGH A POTATO.

No, you don't have to drill a hole in the potato first.

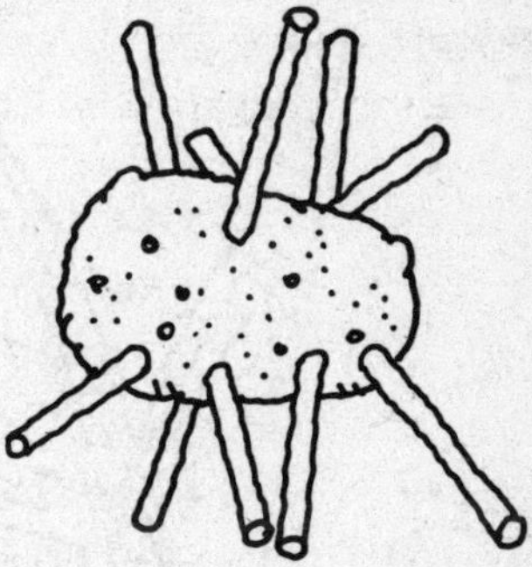

1 All you have to do is put your thumb or forefinger over one end of the straw.

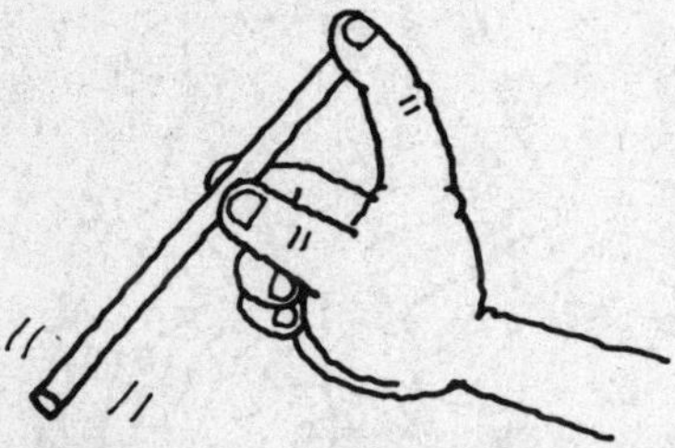

2 Now, with a sharp stabbing movement ram the other end of the straw into the potato. It goes right in and may even be forced out of the other side of the poor spud.

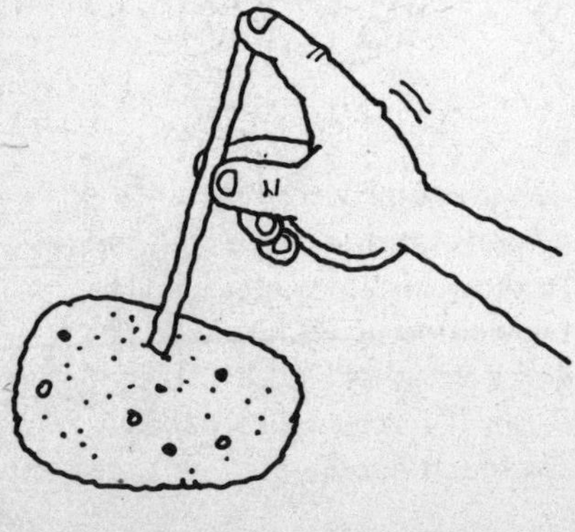

3 Do this enough times and you could eventually chop up a potato.

By sealing up one end of the straw you compress the air inside it, effectively turning it into a strong rod. And that is all you have to do to prove the strength of a straw.

# HOW OFTEN DO YOU HAVE A BATH?

PEOPLE TODAY TAKE BATHS REGULARLY – WHETHER THEY NEED IT OR NOT. BUT PEOPLE IN THE PAST WERE NOT ALWAYS SO CLEAN.

One person noted for her high standards of cleanliness was Elizabeth I who took a bath twice a year!

Other people were not quite so hygienic and as a result tended to smell a little. One solution they came up with was to rub a globe artichoke under their arms. It's very unlikely that this did much good.

Eventually people made pomanders to keep the smells at bay. They were often metal balls containing sweet smelling herbs.

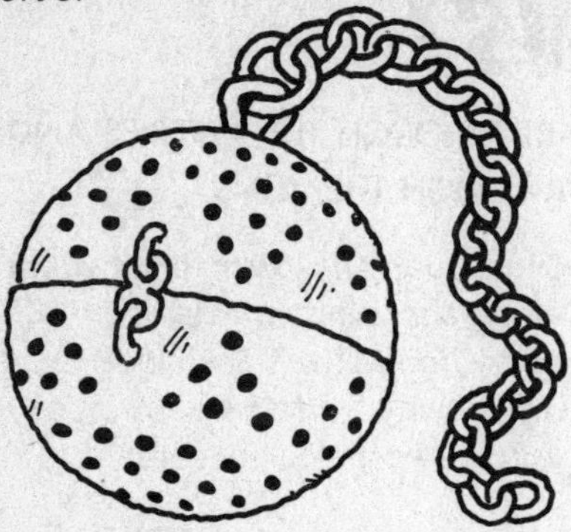

You can make yourself a pomander very easily. It can be used as an alternative to modern air-freshners.

All you need is an orange, some cloves and some ribbon.

1 Tie the ribbon around the orange. This is so that you can hang it up when your pomander is finished.

2 Push as many cloves as possible into the orange. Piercing the skin of the orange releases its lovely smell and this adds to the spicy smell of the cloves.

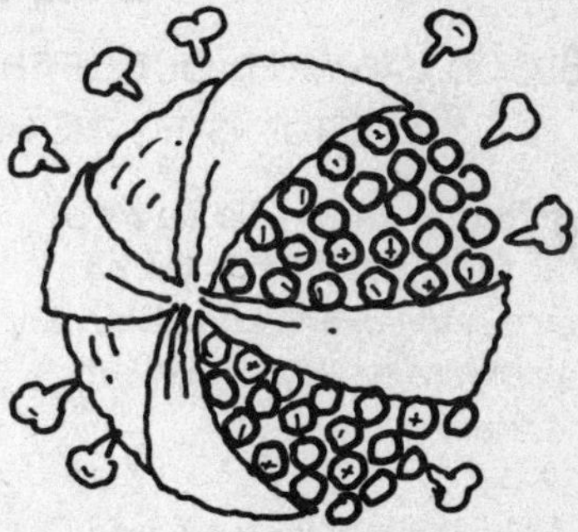

3 To prevent the orange from going off, dust it all over with a mixture of orris root powder and cinnamon. This will preserve the orange for about three weeks.

Carry your pomander around with you for that three weeks and perhaps no-one will notice if you haven't had a bath!

# HOW DO YOU KNOW WHERE YOUR BLOOD FLOWS?

BLOOD IS PUMPED OUT OF THE HEART THROUGH THE ARTERIES AND RETURNS TO THE HEART THROUGH THE VEINS.

We now know this to be a fact, but four hundred years ago no-one knew this and there were several different theories.

In 1616 William Harvey, an English physician, discovered how blood circulated and devised a simple experiment to prove his theory. He showed this experiment to many people, including Charles I to whom he was Royal Physician.

1 Press two fingers together on a prominent vein in your forearm. Now, pressing all the time, push the lower finger down along the vein towards your hand. You will see the blood drain away from the section of vein between your fingers.

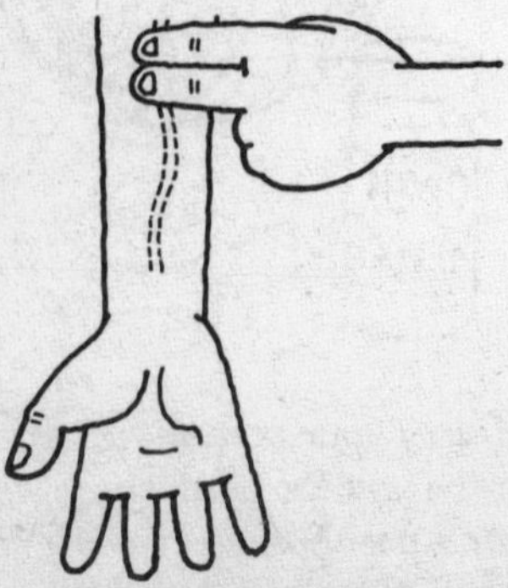

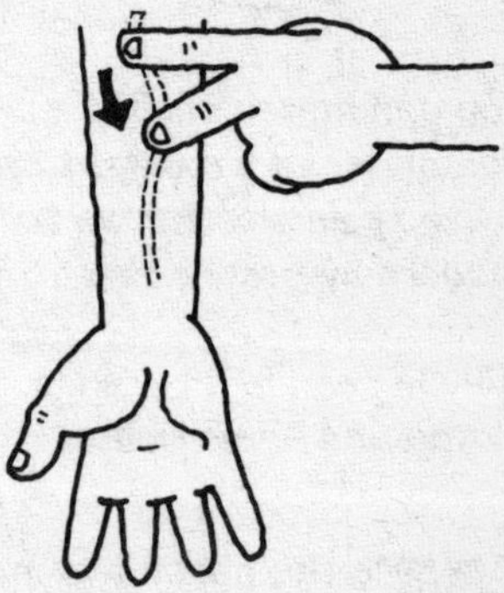

2 Lift the lower finger and blood will flow back into the vein.

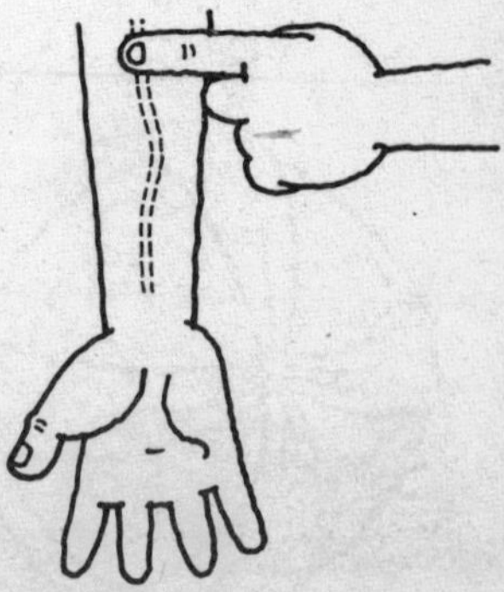

**3** **N**ext try a similar experiment. Place your two fingers on the vein again but this time move the upper fingers upwards along the vein. Once again the blood is drained from the section of vein between your fingers.

**4** **N**ow lift the uppermost finger and you will see that this time the blood does not flow back into the vein.

With this experiment you have shown that the blood is flowing towards the heart. It also shows that your veins have valves in them that prevent the blood from flowing back in the opposite direction.

William Harvey published details of his work on blood in a book called De Motu Cordis in 1627. Many doctors threw scorn on his work but it was not long before others proved he was correct.

Thanks to William Harvey you now know where your blood flows.

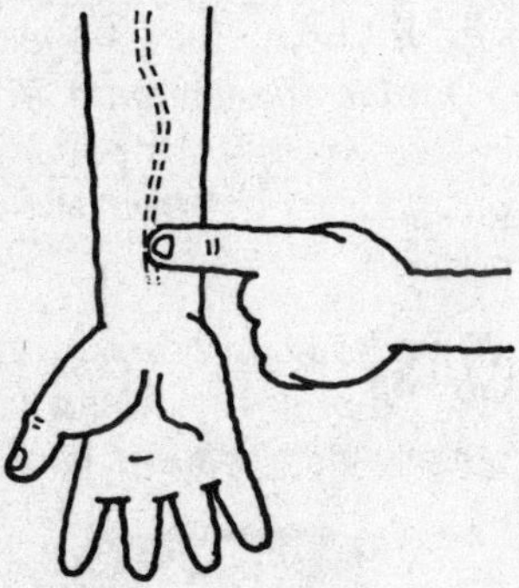

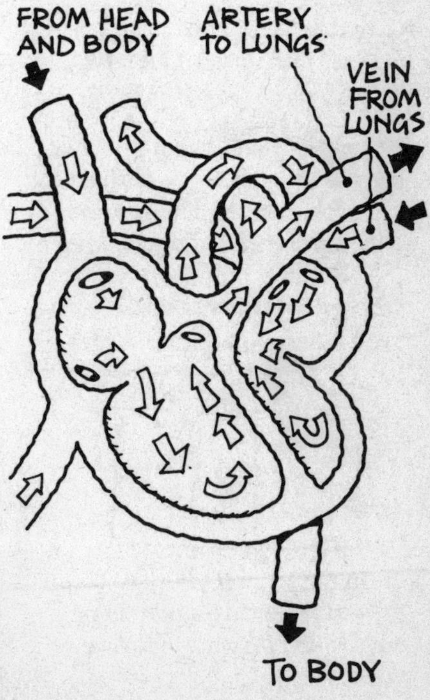

# HOW CAN YOU MAKE SOMEONE LOOK A TOTAL IDIOT?

1 **H**and someone a piece of paper and challenge them to take it in both hands and tear it into three pieces.

No matter how hard they try they will end up with just two pieces.

2 **N**ow hand them another piece of paper – this time with two slits in it. Again your friend will take the edges of the paper,

one in each hand, and try to pull it into three. But again he or she will end up with just two pieces.

If you wish to carry on this torture a little longer you can give them yet another piece of paper with slits that go almost the complete width of the paper – but still they cannot tear it into three.

3 **T**he only way to do it is to cheat. Take a sheet of paper, one edge in each hand, and just before you pull the paper apart put your mouth over the centre portion.

4 **Y**ou can now tear it into three and your friend will look a totally incompetent idiot!

# HOW CAN YOU GROW TWO PLANTS ON ONE PLANT?

TO IMPROVE THE QUALITY OF PLANTS, BOTANISTS OFTEN JOIN TOGETHER TWO DIFFERENT PLANTS TO GET THE BEST QUALITIES OF BOTH OF THEM.

This process is called 'grafting', but it only works using two plants from the same family.

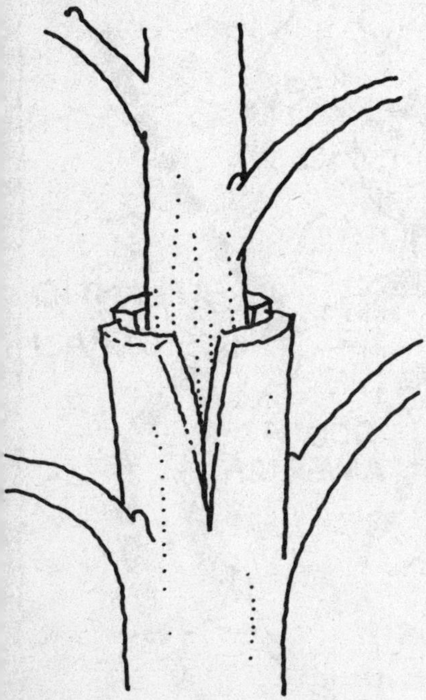

Sometimes this can have amazing results. The potato plant and the tomato plant are members of the same plant family.

If you take a potato plant and cut off the top and replace it with the top of a tomato plant you end up with a plant that bears two different crops.

Below the ground it produces potatoes and above the ground it will bear tomatoes. Sounds like a great space-saving idea for a small garden.

# HOW DID A POSTAGE STAMP CHANGE THE COURSE OF A CANAL?

For hundreds of years sailors had to journey over 11,000 km (7,000 miles) to get from the Atlantic to the Pacific Ocean, even though in Central America they are only 80 km (50 miles) apart.

This was because the 80 km were over land. To get from one ocean to the other meant travelling all the way down the coast of South America, around the dreaded Cape Horn, and then all the way up the other side of South America.

One day someone had a brilliant idea. 'Let's build a canal through Central America.' The great engineer Ferdinand de Lesseps was invited to take on the project. He had recently built the Suez Canal linking the Mediterranean to the Red Sea.

Ferdinand decided to build the canal through the country of Nicaragua. He was very happy with this decision until he received a postcard from a friend in Nicaragua. The stamp showed a volcano. Volcanoes are not the best things to have around major construction projects, so Ferdinand decided to go through Panama instead.

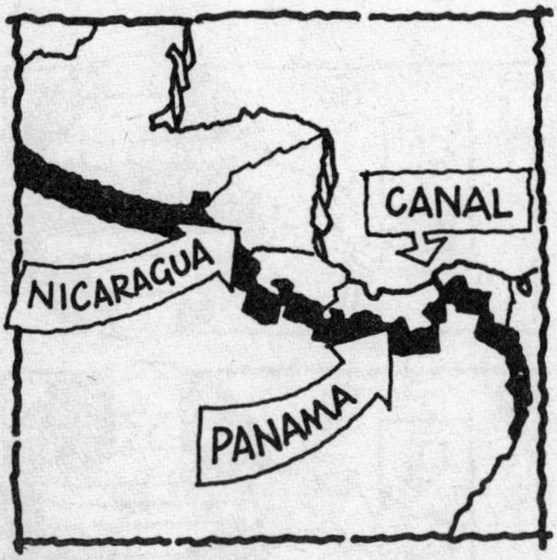


The Panama Canal was started in 1881 but, because de Lesseps ran out of money, it was not completed until 1914. It is now used by more than 11,000 ships every year. And it is where it is all because of a stamp!

# HOW DOES A TOWEL DISPENSER WORK?

WHEN YOU USE A TOWEL DISPENSER IN A WASHROOM IT ALWAYS PROVIDES YOU WITH A LENGTH OF TOWEL TO DRY YOUR HANDS BUT NO MORE.

You can't pull out any more towel without first letting go of the towel and then pulling again.

The secret of how the dispenser does this is two suckers inside the machine.

Pulling the towel down forces the two suckers together. The suckers stick to each other for a while but springs attached to them eventually pull them apart once again.

When the suckers are together the towel mechanism is jammed but once they are apart the towel can be pulled out for another length.

INSIDE THE DISPENSER MECHANISM ▶

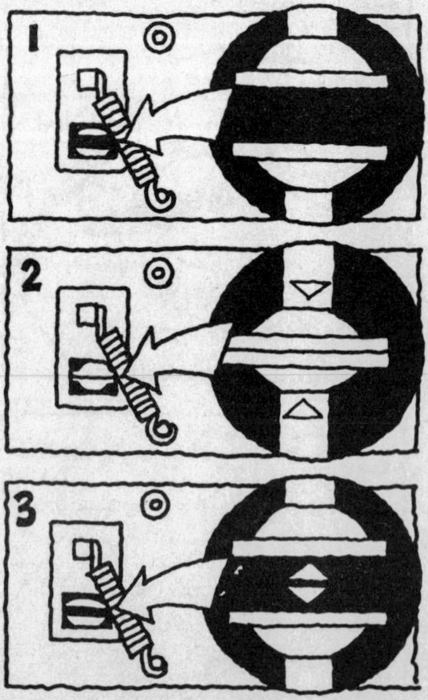

# HOW TO WALK THROUGH NUMBER 10

1 Here is a way to walk through Number 10 Downing Street without getting caught. All you need is a pair of scissors and a postcard of Number 10.

2 Fold the postcard in half lengthways.

3 Now make as many cuts as you can from the central fold to the outer edges and from the outer edges to the central fold. Be careful that you don't cut right through the card as you do this.

Make as many cuts as you possibly can, but make sure that the first and last cuts start from the central fold.

4 Open out the card and cut along the centre fold from the first cut to the last cut.

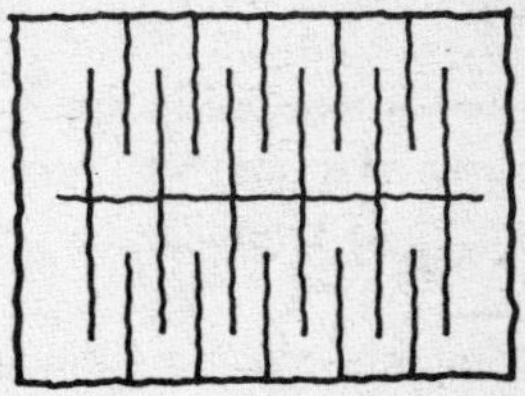

5 Carefully open out the card and form it into a large ring Push your body through this ring and you have managed to walk through Number 10 without getting caught!

# HOW DO YOU MAKE EGG IN TOAST?

**ALL YOU NEED** to make this fabulous dish is a slice of bread, some oil, a frying pan, a grill, an egg and a cup.

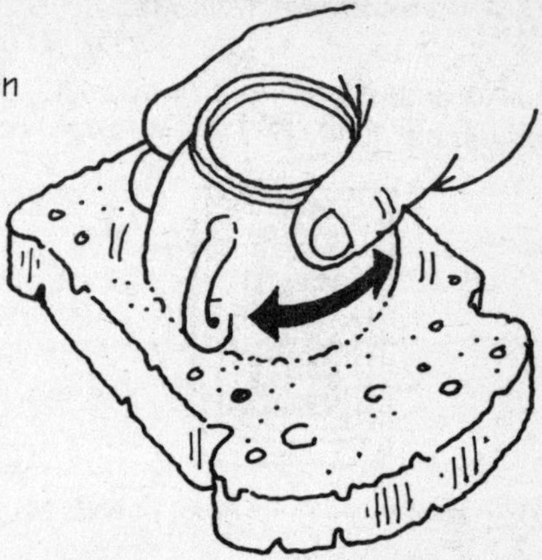

1 Use the cup to make a hole in the centre of the bread. Press the cup, upside down, on the bread and twist to remove the centre of the slice.

It doesn't have to be a circular hole – it can be any shape you like.

2 Put the bread in a frying pan containing some hot oil. Break the egg into the hole. Let some of the egg white go in first to seal the hole.

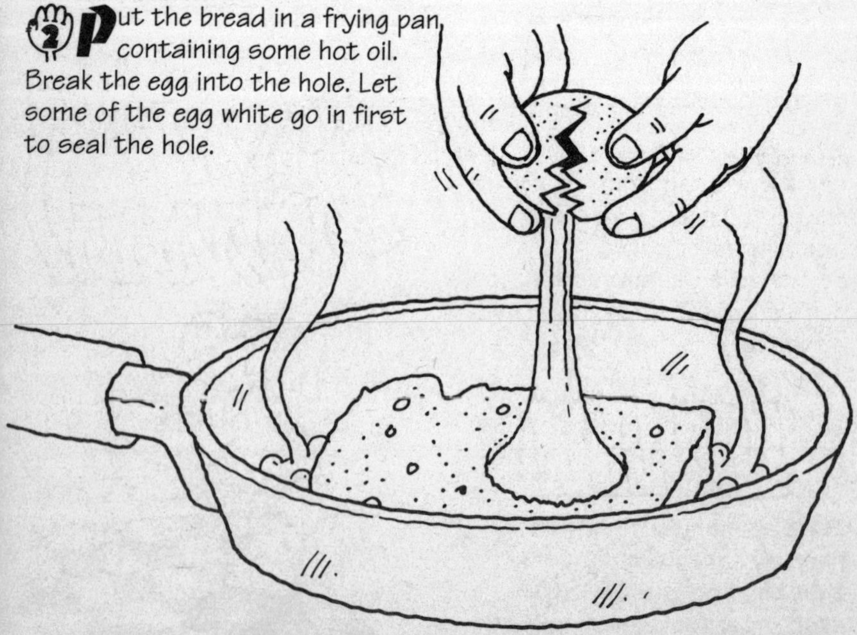

**3** **A**llow the egg to cook most of the way through, then use a spatula to lift the bread (and the egg) out of the pan and onto the grill tray.

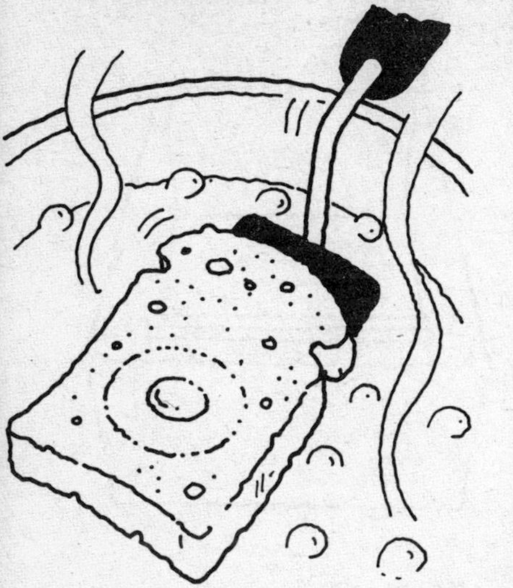

**4** **T**oast the bread under the grill and the top of the egg will get cooked also.

**5** **P**op your egg in toast onto a plate and enjoy a scrumptious breakfast.

# HOW CAN YOU TRAIN A MATCHBOX?

AMAZE YOUR FRIENDS WITH A WONDERFUL PERFORMING MATCHBOX.

1 The secret of this obedient box is inside the tray of the matchbox. Wedge a piece of matchstick across the centre of the tray. This will act like a brake.

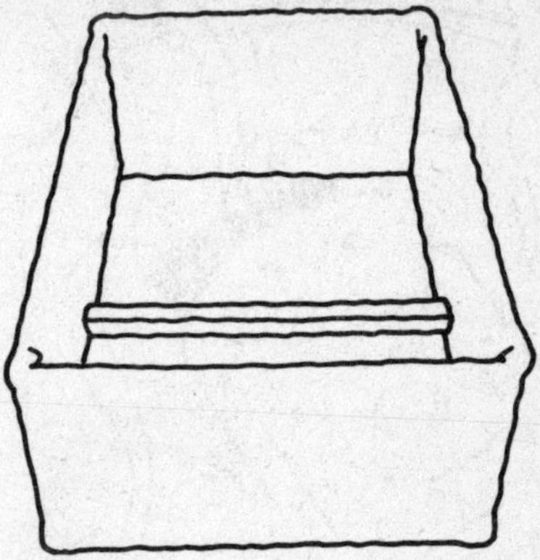

2 Make two holes in the ends of the tray and thread a piece of string through them.

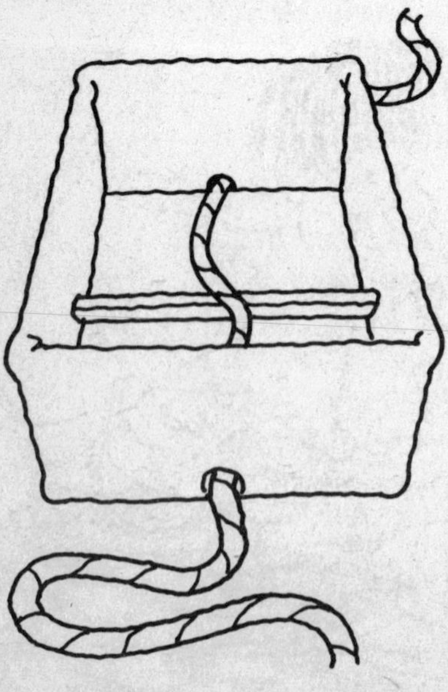

3 Replace the sleeve and practise stopping it as it slides down the length of the string.

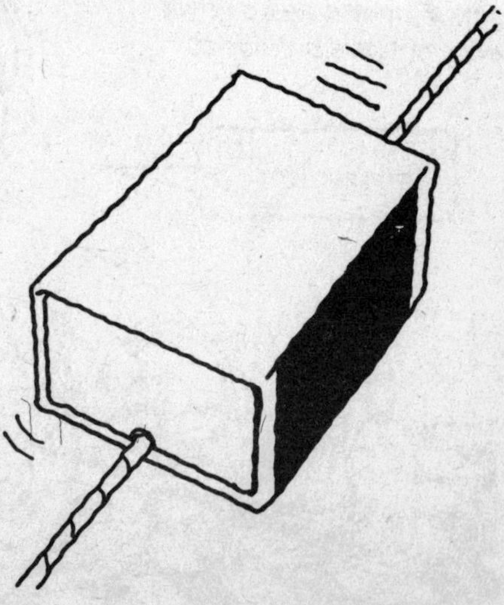

4 If you hold the string fairly loosely in a vertical position, the matchbox naturally slides down to the bottom end of the string. Reverse the position of your hands and the matchbox slides down the string once again. To make the box stop instantly, simply pull the string tight.

5 Now tell your friends that your matchbox is so well trained that it will stop anywhere on the string when someone calls 'stop'. Put the box at the top of the string and let it slide down. When anyone commands the box to stop, pull the string taut and, as if by magic, it will. Do this several times and everyone will be convinced that you really are the proud owner of an intelligent matchbox.

# HOW TO LIFT FIFTEEN NAILS WITH ONE

CHALLENGE A FRIEND TO LIFT 15 BIG NAILS USING JUST ONE OTHER NAIL.

The nails can't be magnetised or glued in any way. The secret is to use long nails with big heads.

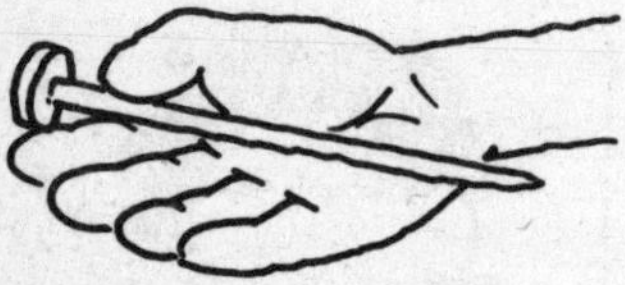

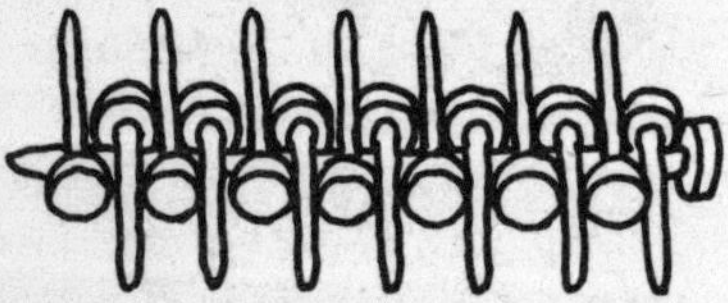

1 Place one nail on the table. Now put 14 nails on top of the first with their head ends lying across it, as shown.

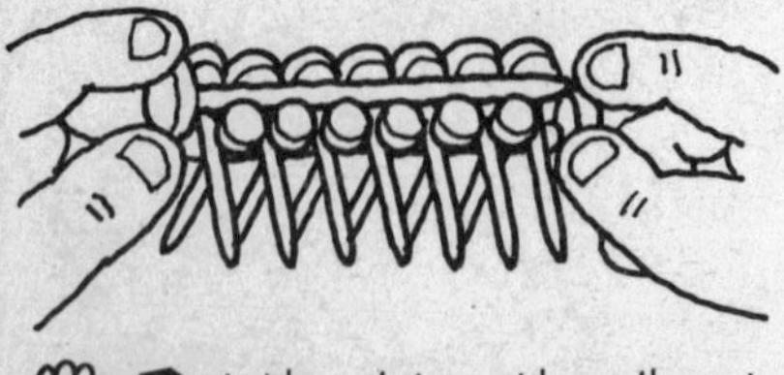

2 Put the sixteenth nail on top of all the others, parallel to the first nail. Hold both the top and bottom nails and lift the whole lot.

At this point your friends may protest that you said you would lift 15 nails with one but that you are using two.

3 Give the nails a slight shake (this puts them all into position) and then let go of the top nail.

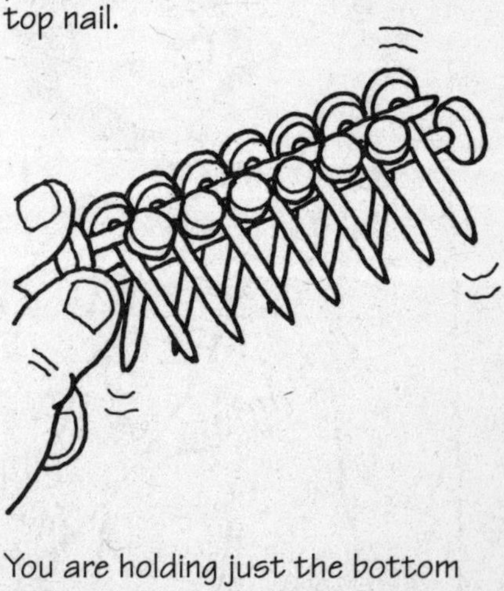

You are holding just the bottom nail and there are 15 others lifted by it. You are a genius!

# HOW CAN A STICK STOP A ROW?

A STICK CAN STOP A ROW IF IT'S A TALLY STICK.

A tally stick is a very old form of keeping note of a debt. Notches were cut in the stick to represent the amount of money owed. The stick was then split down the middle – the debtor kept one half and the creditor kept the other. In this way both people had a record of the amount owing.

When the debtor paid his debt the two tally sticks would be compared. If the number of notches were the same, then both parties knew that everything was fair and above board. If the sticks didn't match, then one of the two people had been doing a little cheating.

And that is how a stick could stop a row.

Tally sticks were the main form of accounting for a very long time, from the days of William the Conqueror up until 1824. They were even used for taxes, the Treasury having one half of the tally stick and the tax payer having the other half.

In 1826, after the system had been changed, orders were given for all the thousands of tally sticks held in the House of Lords for tax purposes to be burned. They were all thrown into a furnace and set alight. Unfortunately, no-one had thought to have the building's chimneys cleaned and the House of Lords burned down.

# HOW CAN WOBBLY WHEELS BE OK?

WOBBLY WHEELS MAY SOUND DANGEROUS, BUT THESE WOBBLY WHEELS ARE EYE-CATCHING FUN.

1 Cut a disc from card and make a hole through its centre. The hole should be big enough to push a pencil through.

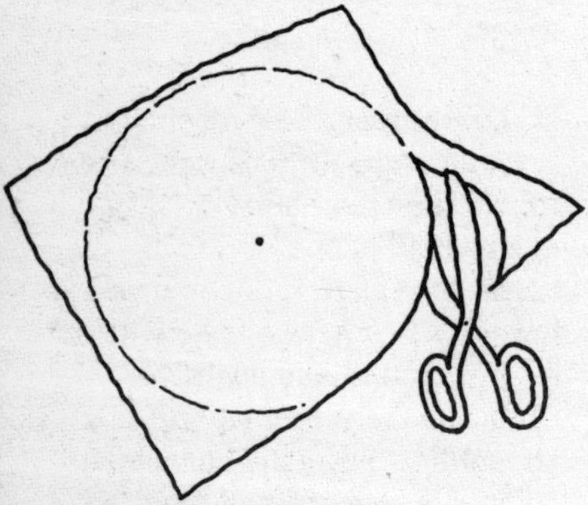

2 Paint a large black circle on the disc, but put it off centre. Paint a smaller disc inside the first with a different centre to the first. Do the same again with a smaller circle still.

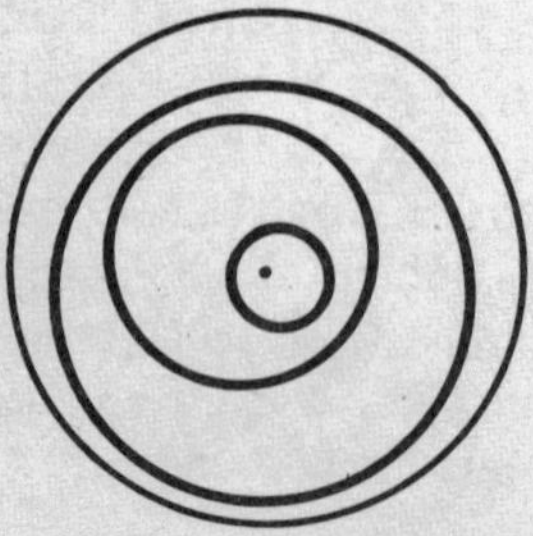

3 Now push a pencil through th central hole and spin the disc. Because your painted circles are off centre you will get the impression that the disc is wobbling.

It is an optical illusion. Your brain is confused by what it sees.

If you have a bicycle with discs on the wheels you could paint them with circles in the same way. When you ride along it will appear that you have wobbly wheels!

# HOW CAN A DOCK LEAF CURE A NETTLE STING?

MOST PEOPLE KNOW THAT RUBBING A DOCK LEAF ON A NETTLE STING GETS RID OF THE STING. IT'S NOT JUST AN OLD WIVES' TALE – IT ACTUALLY WORKS.

The leaf of a nettle is covered with very fine hairs. These hairs are like tiny tubes and they contain poison. When you touch a nettle the hairs get broken and the poison is injected into your skin. As a result your skin gets inflamed and itches.

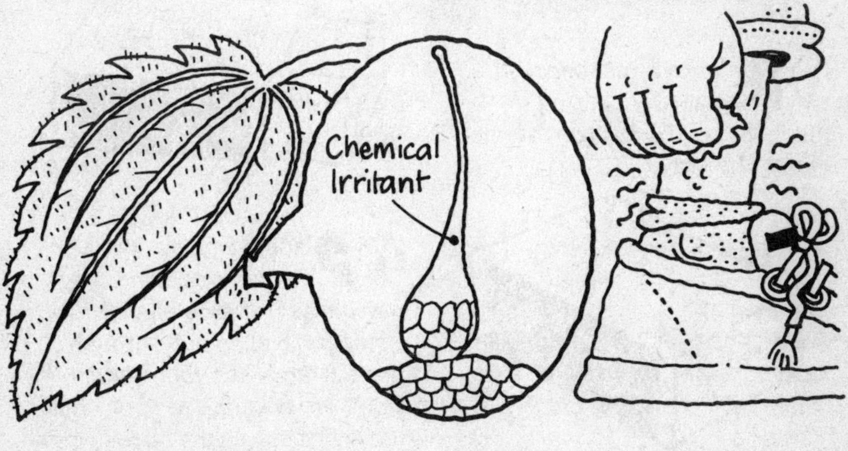


Growing near to a clump of nettles you will often find dock leaves, the ideal cure for nettle stings. All you have to do is grab a dock leaf, crumple it up and rub it on the sting as quickly as you can. It will help relieve the pain.

This happens because the dock leaf draws out the poison injected by the nettle, working rather like a poultice. It also has an astringent quality which causes the skin to tighten and this helps to soothe the area that has been stung.

# HOW CAN YOU TURN 5P INTO 50P?

Show your friends a 5p coin and put it into an empty matchbox.

After a few magic words you open the matchbox and the 5p has changed into a 50p coin. Sounds like a good way of making money!

Actually, it is a cunning magic trick which will stun your friends.

1 Prepare a matchbox in secret by cutting a small slit at the bottom of one end of the tray.

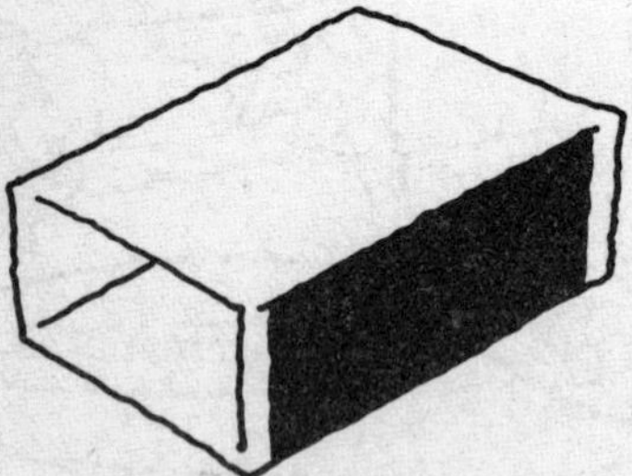

2 Put the tray back into the box but wedge a 50p coin between the top of the tray and the sleeve. You are now ready to show the trick.

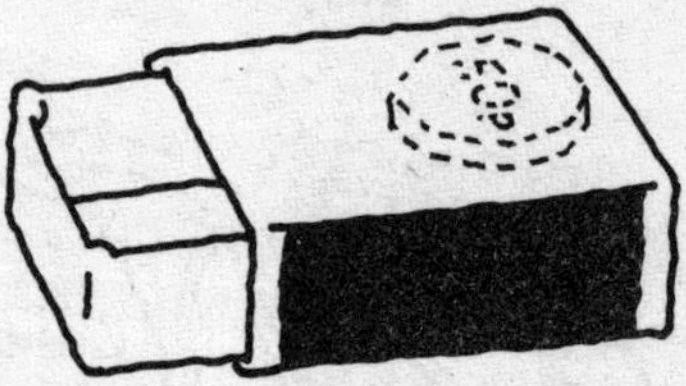

3 Place a 5p coin into the tray. As you close the tray tip the matchbox upwards slightly. The 5p coin will slide out through the slit and into your hand. Don't let anyone see your hand move or they might guess what has happened.

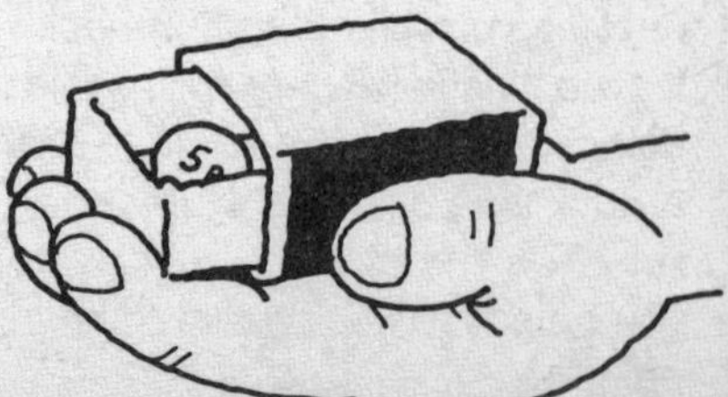

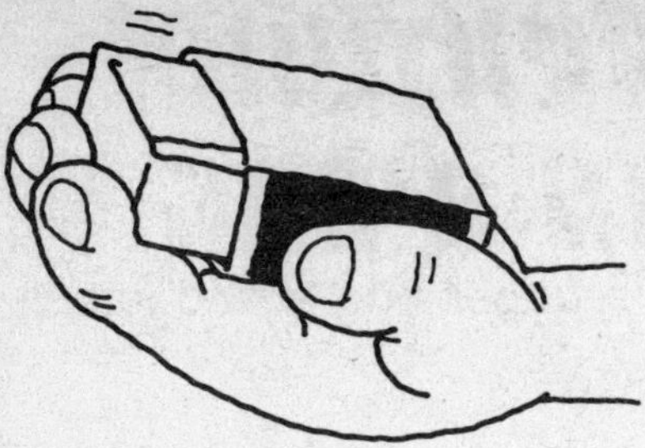

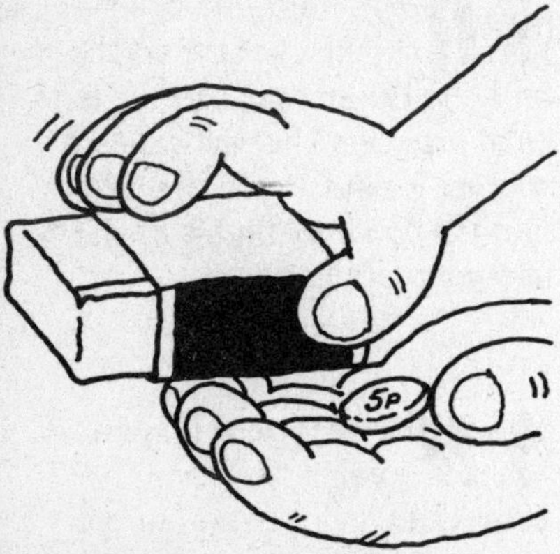


**4** **A**s you close the drawer the 50p is forced from its secret hiding place and into the drawer. Now say a few magic words.

**5** **W**hen you open the box the 5p piece will have magically turned into 50p. Show the 50p, as you put the box and the secretly held 5p into your pocket.

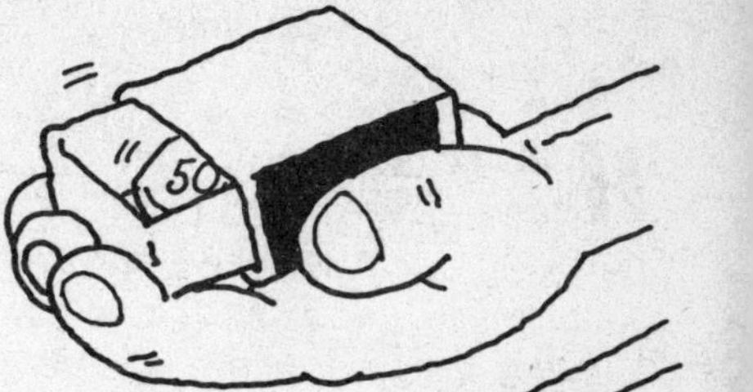


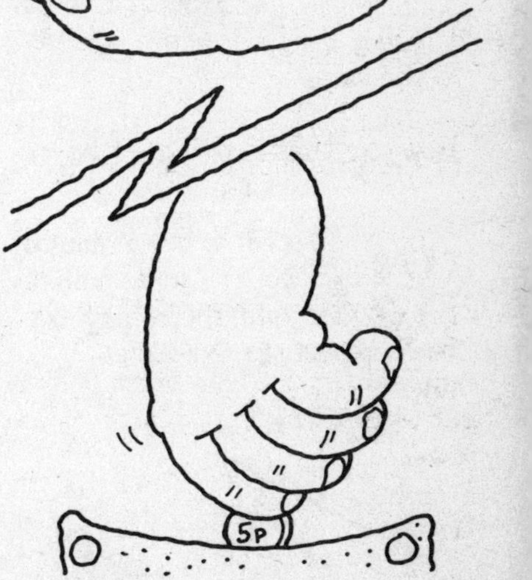

# HOW TO CATCH NOTHING IN A BAG

**ALL YOU NEED** for this trick is a paper bag – and lots of nothing.

Hold the bag in your right hand. Grab a fistful of nothing in your left hand, throw it in the air ... and catch it in the bag. Everyone hears it land in the bag!

How can that be? Here's how.

1 The secret is being able to click your fingers. Push the ball of your right thumb against the top pad of the second finger.

2 Press hard and then let the thumb click off to the right and the finger towards the left. With practise this will cause a clicking sound. If you are left handed you may find it easier to use your left hand.

3 Now click your fingers while holding the paper bag in your hand. It looks and sounds as if something has dropped in the bag.

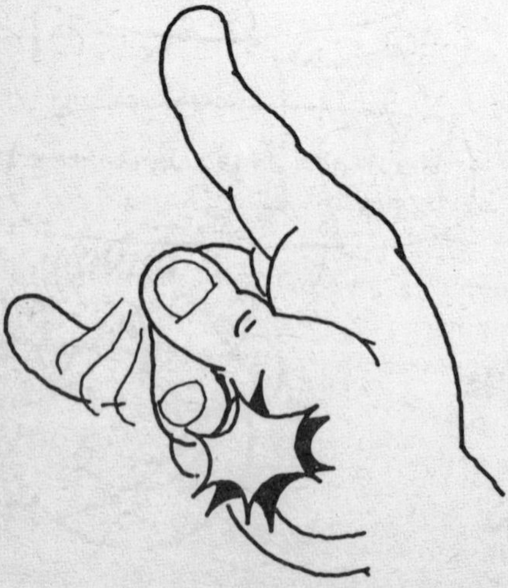

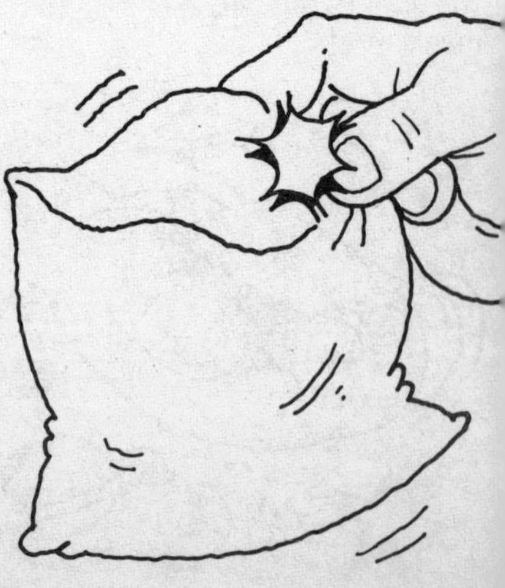

**4** **R**each into the air with your left hand. Grab a handful of nothing. Throw it towards the bag. Secretly click your fingers . . . and it appears that you have caught nothing in a paper bag.

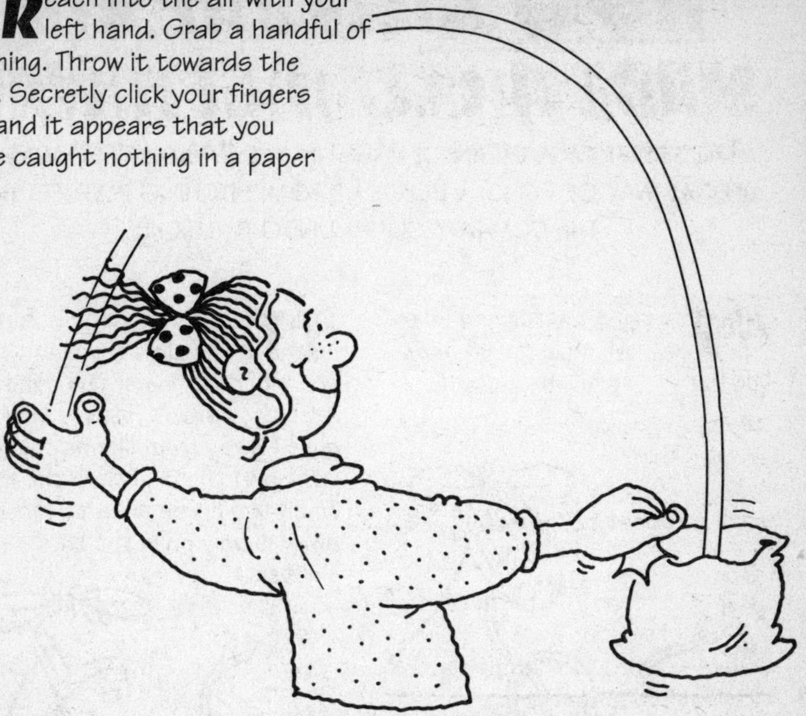

**5** **I**f you are really clever hold a bag in each hand. Get someone to throw two handfuls of nothing towards you and catch one lot in each bag.

# HOW BILLY THE KID MADE A CLEAN GETAWAY

THE SECRET OF A CLEAN GETAWAY IN THE 'WILD WEST' WAS A SPECIAL WAY OF TYING A HORSE UP TO A HITCHING POST SO THAT THE COWBOY COULD UNDO IT QUICKLY.

1 The reins are formed into a loop which is pulled under the bar of the hitching post.

2 A second loop is formed further along the rein and this is pushed through the first loop.

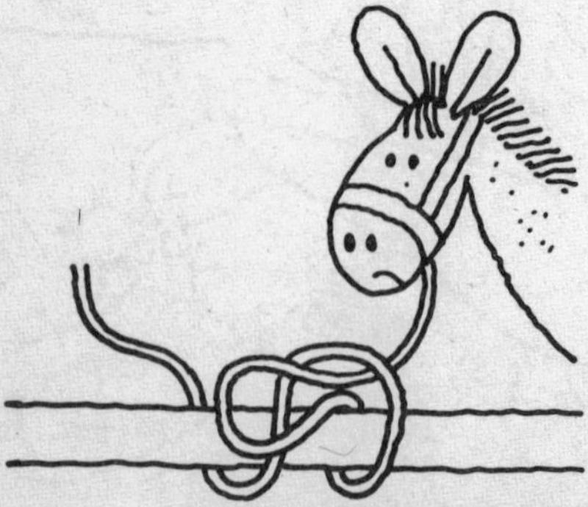

3 Then a third loop is formed and pulled through the second loop. One of the reins near the horse's head is then pulled away from the hitching post and this tightens the knot. When the horse tries to move away it only pulls the knot tighter.

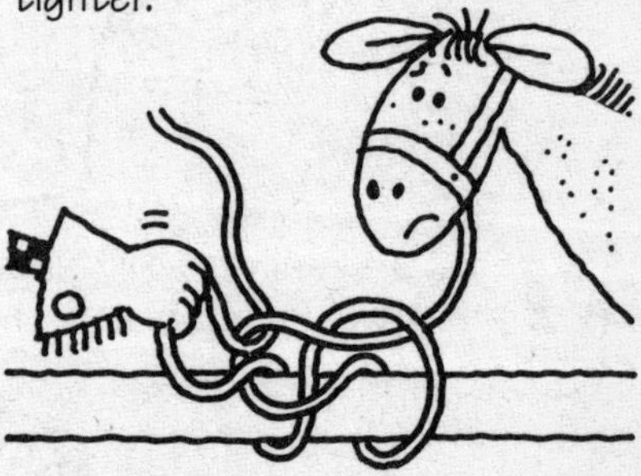

4 To free the horse the cowboy only has to pull the other en of the rein and the knot is instantly undone.

# HOW DO BAR CODES WORK?

WHEN YOU BUY SOMETHING FROM A SHOP YOU WILL NOTICE A NUMBER OF BLACK AND WHITE LINES ON IT. THIS IS A BAR CODE.

The checkout operators in shops run scanners over bar codes. This sends a message to a computerised till which then says how much money you have to pay.

5 000128 285971

But how does the scanner read the code? The scanner gives out light, just like a torch. When the scanner is passed over the black and white lines, the black areas reflect less light back into the scanner than the white bits.

At the beginning of the bar code is a start mark. This tells the scanner that it is reading a bar code and not a passing zebra.

The widths of the black and white lines of the code give the scanner the numbers of the code and the price. A stop mark at the end of the bar code signals the end of the code.

The computer then reads the price and all you have to do is pay the bill!

# HOW DO YOU PLAY THE DIDGERIDOO?

THE DIDGERIDOO IS AN INSTRUMENT USED BY THE AUSTRALIAN ABORIGINES, THAT IS THE NATIVE AUSTRALIANS.

It is made from the branch of a eucalyptus tree. Running through the middle of the branch is a long hole which is made by termites burrowing from one end to the other.

One end of the instrument is placed to the lips. A raspberry-like sound is made by the lips and this gets amplified by the instrument.

It takes a lot of puff to play the didgeridoo so the player has to learn what is known as circular breathing. This is a technique of drawing in air through the nose while at the same time exhaling air through the mouth.

To practise circular breathing for yourself take a mouthful of water from a glass. Now slowly expel the water from your mouth in a continuous stream. Take a long sniff through your nose at the same time. If you can breath in through your nose at the same time as blowing air out of your mouth, you have achieved circular breathing.

All you need now is a didgeridoo.

# HOW OLD ARE YOUR MARBLES?

MARBLES GO BACK A VERY LONG WAY.

People in the 16th century played with cherry stones. After eating the cherries they spat the stones into a 'cherry pit', a hole in the ground. The great British playwright William Shakespeare mentions this in his play *Twelfth Night*.

But marbles are even older than that!

The ancient Greeks played a game with nuts called Omilla. The players had to knock nuts out of a circle. If this happened the player kept the nuts he'd won.

But marbles are even older than that!

In the days of the Pharaohs, the ancient Egyptians played with marbles made of clay. They rolled them through pillars and scored points.

But marbles are even older than that!!!

Cavemen played marbles with perfectly smooth, perfectly round pebbles. They made the pebbles round by leaving them in streams and rivers until the water smoothed them into perfect marbles!

And that's how old marbles are!

# HOW CAN YOU MAKE PAPER PERFORM ACROBATICS?

1 Write a secret message on a sheet of paper. Show the blank side to a friend and bet that you can show the message without turning the paper over.

2 Fold the paper in half, making the fold towards your body.

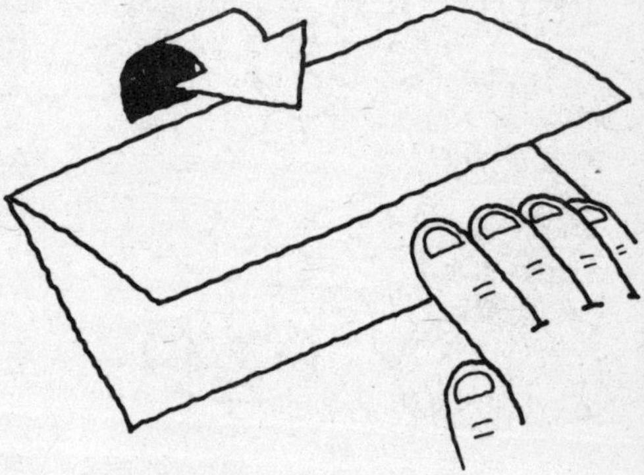

3 Fold the paper in half again. Again this fold must be towards you.

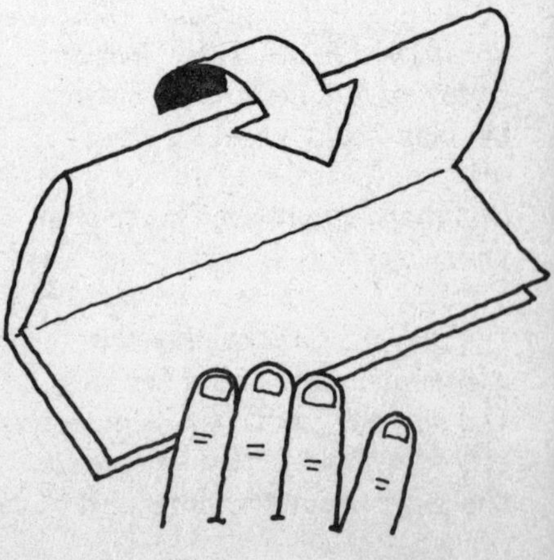

4 Next fold the paper in half from left to right.

5 Now unfold the paper. Unfold the first fold from the bottom.

6 Unfold the last fold downwards.

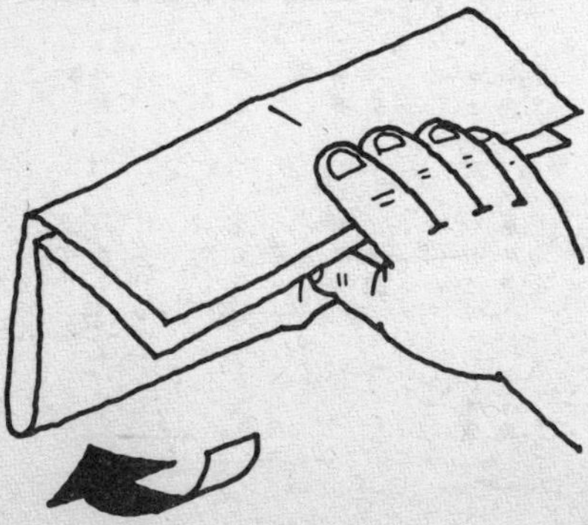

7 Unfold the next fold upwards.

8 The message on the back of the paper is now revealed without turning the paper over.

That's how to make paper perform acrobatics.

# HOW DO BLIND PEOPLE READ AND WRITE?

BLIND PEOPLE USE TOUCH TO READ AND WRITE.

It's a system known as Braille, named after its inventor Louis Braille. Louis Braille was himself blinded at the age of three when he had an accident in his father's workshop in Coupvrayn, near Paris.

Braille is a system of six raised dots. By learning the various combinations of dots, a blind person can read the letters. It is used in books, on board games, tape measures, labels and for many other things.

Special machines enable people to write in Braille.

Nowadays, computers are used to produce Braille. Blind people can even read what is on the computer by small pins that come up through a display board. Modern computers can even voice what is on the screen and a scanner can be used to transfer ordinary writing into the computer.

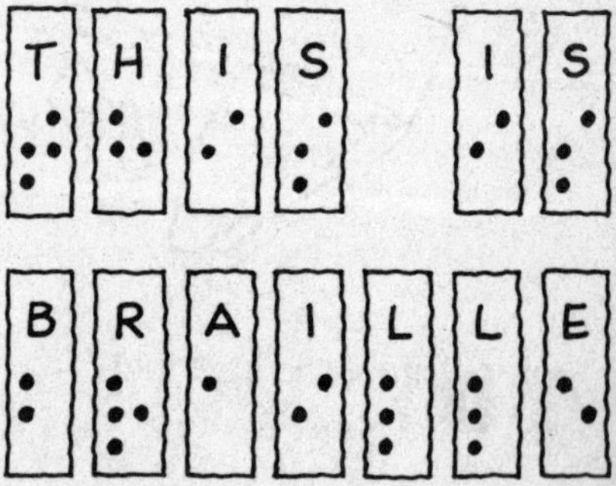


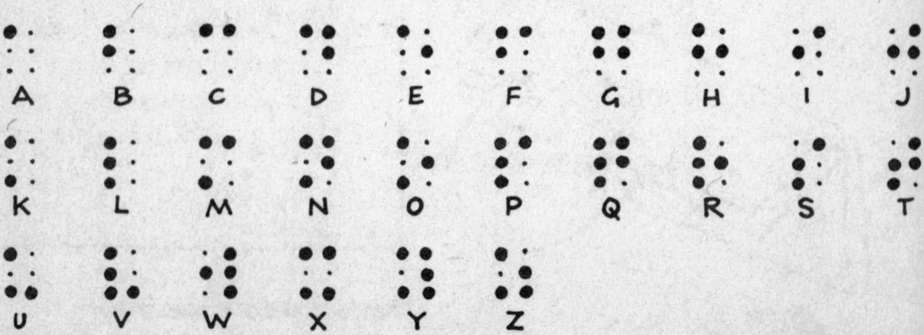

# HOW DO MARIONETTES MOVE?

MARIONETTES ARE PUPPETS WORKED BY STRINGS.

These strings are attached to the various parts of the marionette's jointed body. The other ends of the strings are fixed to control bars.

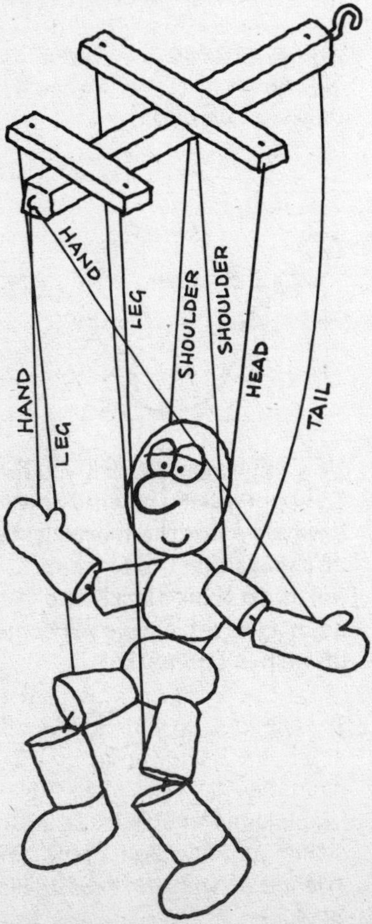

By tipping or lifting the control bars the puppeteer raises or lowers the strings and these move the puppet's jointed limbs.

To make the strings invisible they are first coated with an 'anti-glare' substance and then they are painted to match the background.

# HOW CAN YOU READ MINDS?

TRY THIS FOR YOURSELF FIRST.

1. **T**hink of any number between one and ten.

   7

2. **M**ultiply it by nine.

   7 × 9 = 63

3. **A**dd the two digits of your answer together

   6 + 3 = 9

4. **A**dd three.

   9 + 3 = 12

5. **N**ow divide by three.

   12 ÷ 3 = 4

6. **Y**ou should now have a single digit number. Count through the alphabet to the letter at that number. In other words, if your answer is one the letter you choose is A. If the answer is two your letter is B. Three = C, 4 = D, 5 = E, 6 = F, 7 = G, and so on.

7. You should now be thinking of a letter. Now as quickly as you can, write down the name of a country beginning with the letter you are thinking of.

8. **L**et's see . . . ah, yes . . . the country you have written down is Denmark.

How did I know? Well if you follow the sum given, the answer will always be 4 – the fourth letter of the alphabet is D – and asked to think quickly the country most people will come up with is Denmark.

Try this out on your friends. If by any chance they come up with countries like Dominica, the Dominican Republic or Djibouti either you have some very clever friends or they have read this book.

# HOW DOES A HOVERCRAFT WORK?

A HOVERCRAFT WORKS BY FLOATING ON A CUSHION OF AIR.

To make a model to show how it works, you will need a margarine tub, a cotton reel and a balloon.

1 Make a hole in the bottom of the margarine tub, then fix all the bits together like this:

When Christopher Cockerell invented the hovercraft in 1954, he didn't experiment with a balloon, a cotton reel and a margarine tub. He used a hairdryer and a coffee tin. Later he added another coffee tin inserted inside the first. This made the downward air-flow more controllable and it produced much more lift.

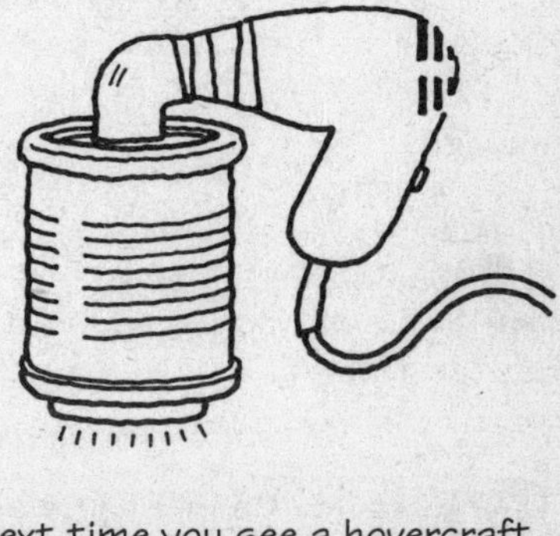

2 Blow up the balloon and pinch the end together with your fingers. Then place the contraption down on a table letting go of the balloon. You will see that as air escapes from the balloon it lifts your 'hovercraft' up from the table.

Next time you see a hovercraft, just remember that it started as a hairdryer and a coffee tin.

# HOW OLD ARE EASTER EGGS?

THE IDEA OF GIVING SWEET EASTER EGGS ONLY GOES BACK A HUNDRED YEARS OR SO WHEN PEOPLE STARTED GIVING EACH OTHER MARZIPAN EGGS.

Long before that people gave each other real eggs, dyed in a variety of colours. These were known as pace eggs.

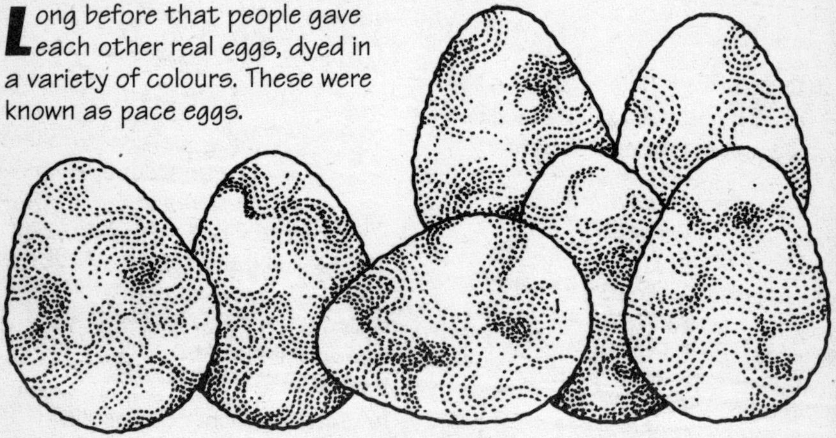

Giving eggs as present in the spring goes back nearly 3000 years. Way back in 900 BC, the Chinese gave each other eggs painted scarlet. So the Easter egg is even older than the custom of Easter itself!

Make your own pace egg to give someone as a special Easter gift.

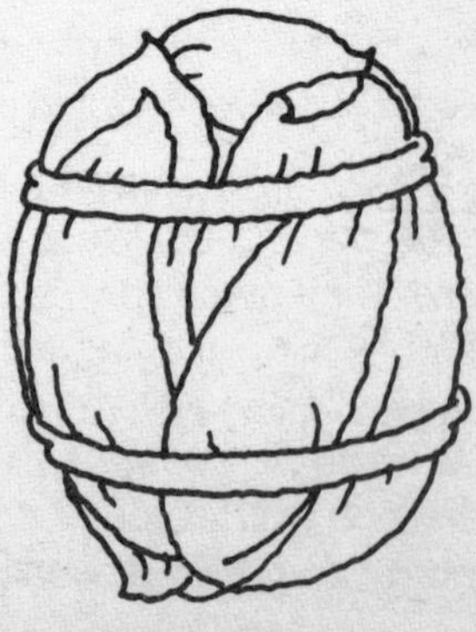

1 Take an ordinary egg and cover it with an onion skin. Use a rubber band or two to hold the onion skin in place.

**2** Get an old stocking and cut off the foot (getting permission first, of course).

**3** Drop the egg into the stocking foot and tie a knot over the top of it.

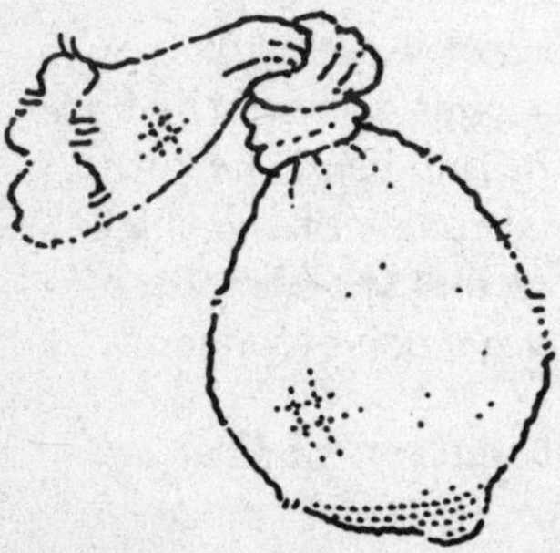

**4** Carefully lower the egg into a pan of boiling water, taking care not to get your hand too near the steam or the water itself. Leave it in the boiling water for ten minutes.

**5** Haul the egg out of the water, taking great care how you handle it because it will be very hot.

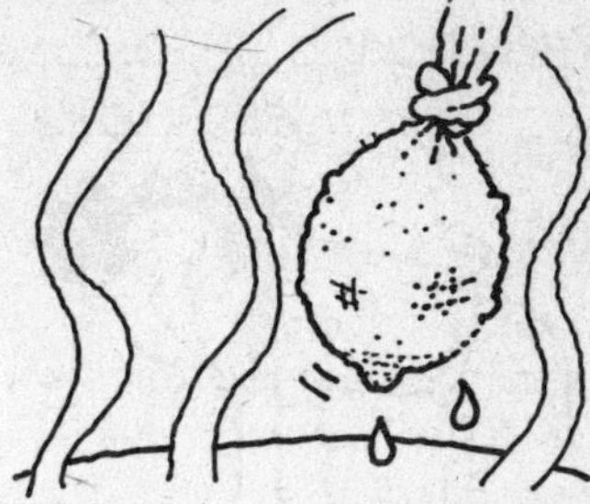

**6** When it has cooled, remove the egg from the stocking and take off the onion skin. Your egg should now be covered with a lovely marbled effect. Dry it off and rub a little cooking oil over it to give it a shine.

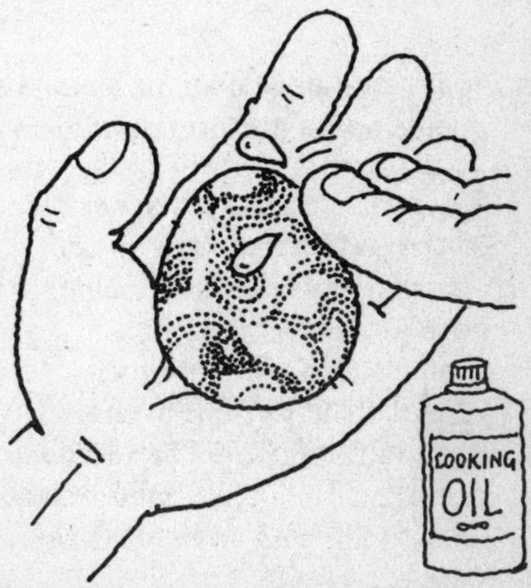


By adding food colouring to the water you can get different effects.

# HOW CAN YOU LIFT AN AUSTRALIAN?

WHEN PICKING UP SOMETHING, MOST PEOPLE BEND FROM THE WAIST, KEEPING THEIR LEGS STRAIGHT.

This is the wrong way to lift anything as it puts all the strain on the lower back muscles which are relatively weak.

The correct way to lift something is to keep the back straight and bend the knees. This makes use of the thigh muscles and the shoulders which are much stronger.

To lift an Australian, or anyone else for that matter, medical people use a method developed in Australia.

Two people stand on either side of the patient seated on the side of the bed. One shoulder goes under the patient's armpits and the arm goes beneath the patient's legs. Both nurses clasp their hands together. The other hand should rest on the bed to help lift up.

The patient, who is facing the opposite direction to the two lifters, can now be lifted easily.

# HOW DO YOU RACE RAISINS?

RACING RAISINS IS AN EXCITING TABLE-TOP GAME THAT YOU CAN PLAY WITH YOUR FRIENDS. ALL YOU NEED ARE SOME RAISINS AND A JUG OF LEMONADE.

1 Drop two raisins into the lemonade and they will sink to the bottom. This is because the raisins are heavier than the lemonade. Does that sound raisinable?

2 Gradually some of the bubbles of the lemonade will stick to the wrinkles on the raisins. This will make the raisins buoyant and they will float to the surface.

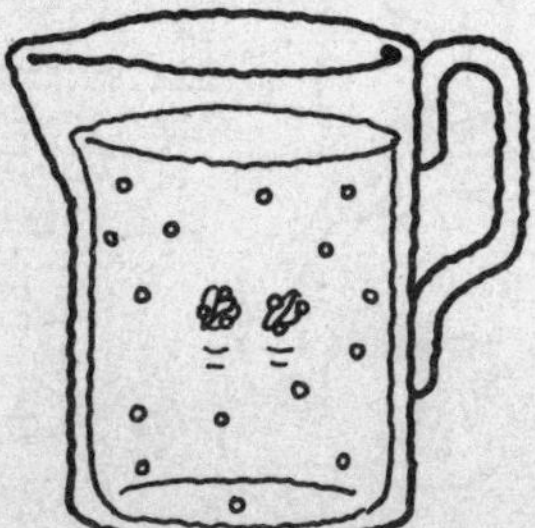

3 When the raisins reach the surface the bubbles burst and the raisins sink to the bottom again.

4 Each trip down to the bottom and up to the top counts as one circuit. Before the race decide upon the number of circuits to be raced and the first raisin to complete that number is the winner.

# HOW CAN 12 DIVIDED BY 2 EQUAL 7?

EVERYONE KNOWS THAT 12 DIVIDED BY 2 EQUALS 6. BUT YOU CAN PROVE THAT 12 DIVIDED BY 2 EQUALS 7.

This is how.

1 The Roman numeral for 12 is XII. Get some dead matches and form this number with eight of them.

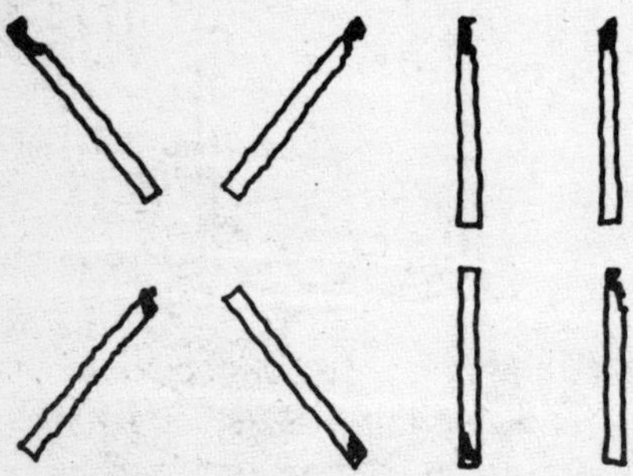

2 Dividing by two is the same as halving a number. Half your Roman twelve by drawing an imaginary horizontal line through it.

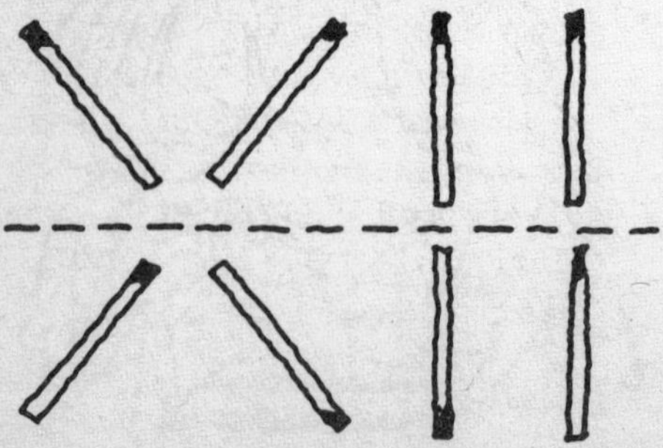

3 Remove the matches from t lower half.

You are now left with four matches that form the Roman number VII and VII is seven. So you have proved that twelve divided by two equals seven.

Simple when you know how!

# HOW PENDULUMS SAVE LIVES

BELIEVE IT OR NOT, PENDULUMS SAVE MILLIONS OF LIVES EVERY DAY.

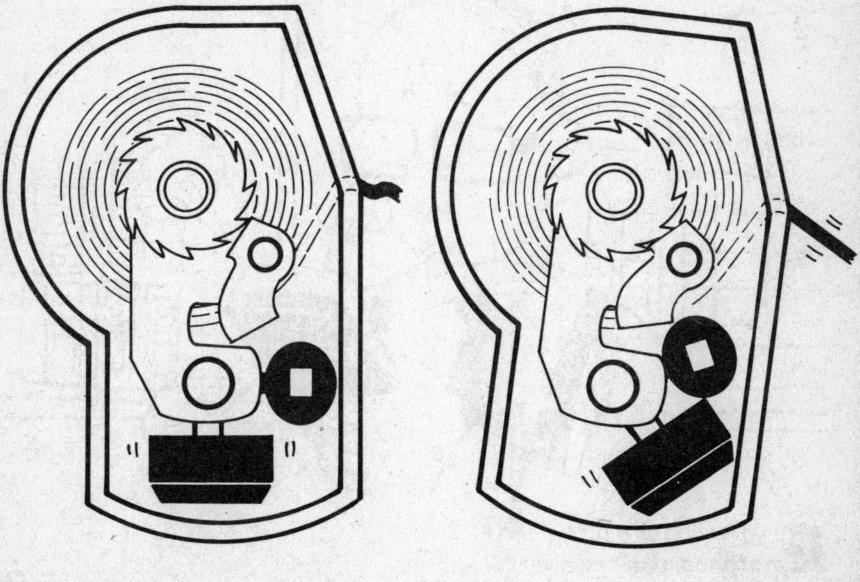

This is because the main part of the inertia-reel seat-belt used in cars is a pendulum.

The inertia seat-belt allows you to move around freely in your seat and adjust your position. But if the car is forced to stop suddenly and you shoot forwards, the seat-belt locks tight to stop you crashing forward.

Inside the seat-belt mechanism is a swinging pendulum. When the car is moving the pendulum swings slightly. But if the car stops suddenly the pendulum swings further and hits against a lever which jams the seat-belt in position and holds the person safely in the car.

# HOW TO MAKE A PROFIT

If you have nine items and you can turn them into ten you have made a profit of one. Business people struggle every day to do this. You can do it very easily.

All you need are nine dead matches, pens or even sticks.

This is how you make those nine items into ten, thus making a profit.

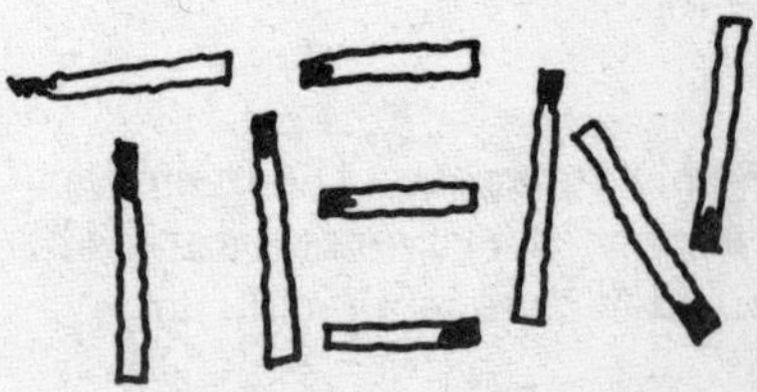

Simply lay out the nine items like this . . . and you have made ten.

If you could do this with money you'd be a millionaire in no time!

# HOW DO YOU WRAP A SARI?

A SARI IS A LENGTH OF MATERIAL DRAPED AROUND THE BODY.
IT IS TRADITIONALLY WORN BY INDIAN WOMEN.
MAKE YOUR OWN SARI.

1 Get about six metres of material. Start by tucking one end of the sari into the top of a petticoat.

2 Keep tucking it in all the way round your body.

3 The end of the sari, the bola, goes under the left arm then round the back and under the right arm. It is then flicked over the left shoulder where it can be secured with a brooch.

Most saris are worn like this although there are some regional variations.

# HOW DID A STICK SAVE AN ARMY?

2400 YEARS AGO IN ANCIENT GREECE THE SPARTANS FOUGHT A WAR AGAINST THE INVADING PERSIANS.

Often the Spartans wanted to get messages from their headquarters to the leaders in the front line. But they were aware that Persian spies might intercept these messages, so they had to send them in secret.

To do this they devised a cunning coding device ... a stick. But to secret coders it is not a stick but a skitali.

You can use the same method to send secret messages to your friends.

1. Cut two pieces from an old broom handle. You have one piece and give the other to a friend.

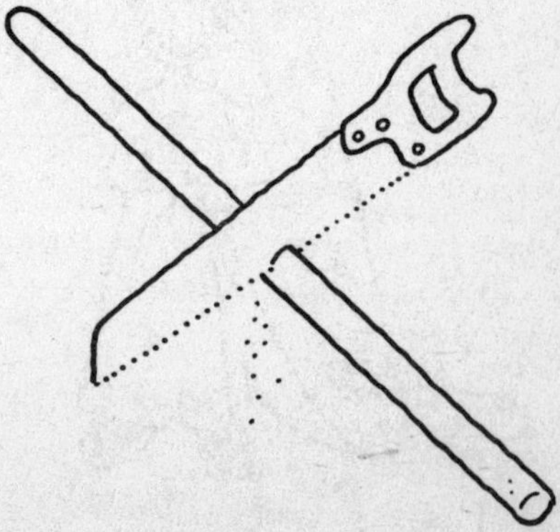

2 Get a long narrow strip of paper and wrap it around your skitali (broom handle).

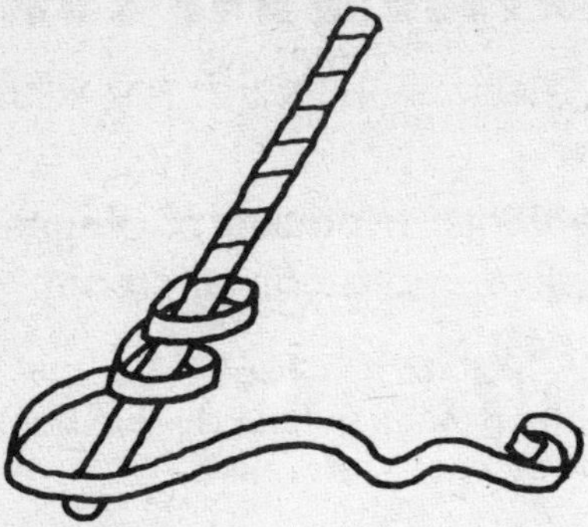

3 Now write your message down the strip, a letter to each level, as shown.

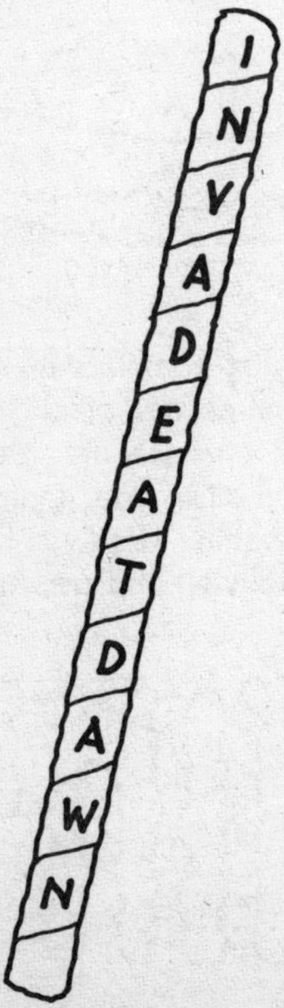


4 Unwrap the paper and write lots of other letters all over it. Anyone looking at the piece of paper will only see only a mass of jumbled letters. The only way to unscramble the code is to use a duplicate skitali.

5 When your friend receives your secret message he or she has to wrap the strip around their skitali and, because it is the same size as the first skitali, the message is automatically revealed.

# HOW TO MAKE A GINGERNUT SANDWICH

IF YOU ARE SWEET TOOTHED THIS COULD BE THE THING FOR YOU.

**YOU WILL NEED** just three ingredients: a packet of ginger-nut biscuits, a bowl of orange juice and a can of cream.

In addition to these ingredients there are just three actions to remember: dunking, squirting and squashing.

1 First, dunk all the gingernut biscuits in the orange juice.

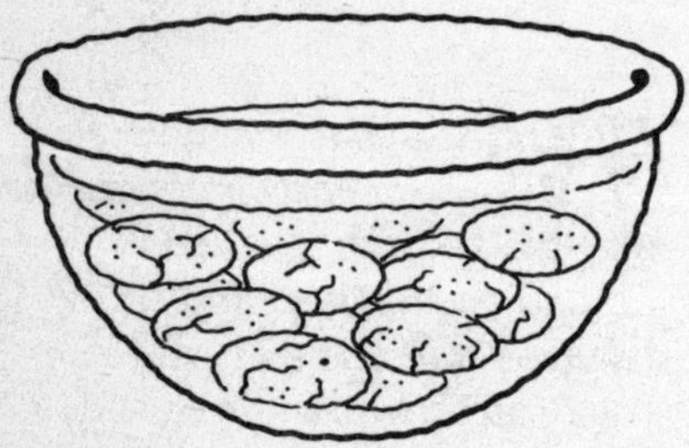

2 After just half a minute, take out a biscuit and squirt (the second action) some cream onto the biscuit.

3 Take another biscuit and squash (the third action) it against the cream.

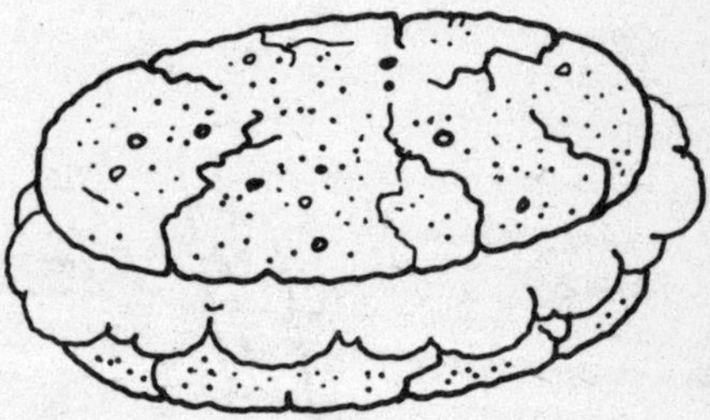

4 Squirt some cream against the second biscuit and then press another biscuit against it. Continue like this, squirting and squashing, until you have a row of biscuits and cream.

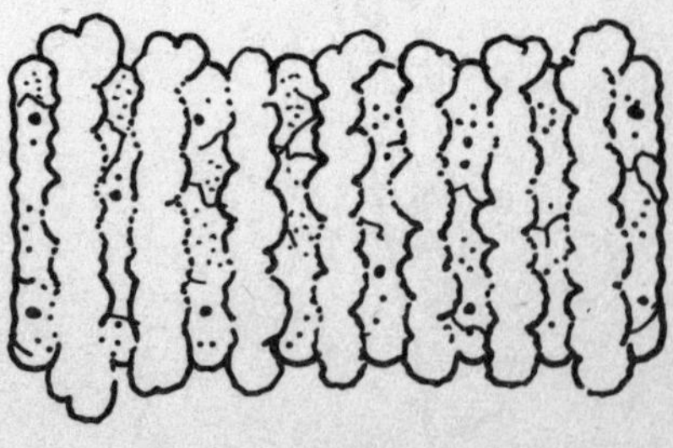

**5** **N**ow cover the whole concoction with cream. If you want to, use a spatula to smooth out the surface of the cream.

**6** **N**ow for the cooking. This is a dish you cook in the fridge. Just put your creamy, gingery, orangey confection in the fridge for about an hour.

When you can wait no longer bring it out of the fridge and give everyone a generous portion of your scrummy gingernut sandwich.

# HOW TO ACHIEVE THE IMPOSSIBLE

YOU SIMPLY CAN'T ACHIEVE THE IMPOSSIBLE. BUT THIS SEEMS IMPOSSIBLE AND IT WORKS!

1 Take two tumblers and immerse them in a bowl of water. Keep the tumblers under the water as you place them mouth to mouth.

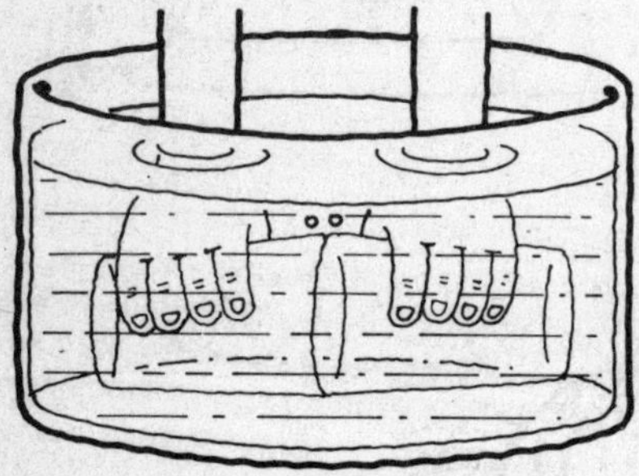

2 Now turn the tumblers to a vertical position, still mouth to mouth, and bring them out of the water.

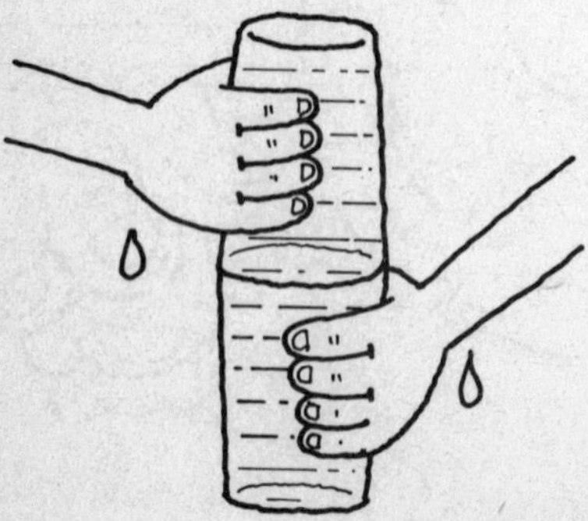

3 Place them on a deep tray (just in case you spill any water).

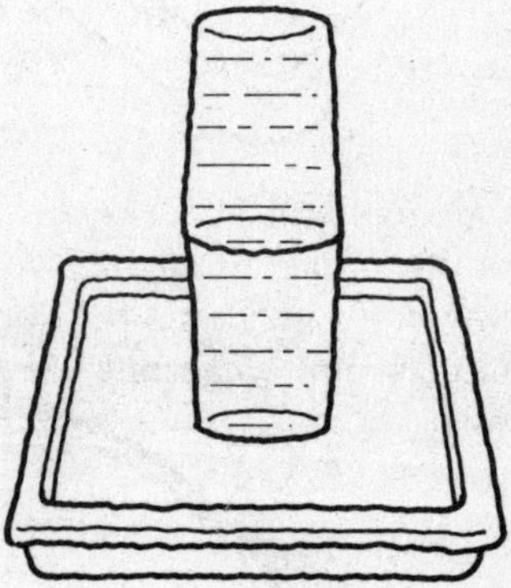

The problem now is how to raise the top glass without the water pouring out. Impossible? Not if you know how!

Take a coin and very carefully push it between the rims of the two glass tumblers. Once you have got the coin into position there will obviously be a gap between the two tumblers, but the water won't come gushing out.

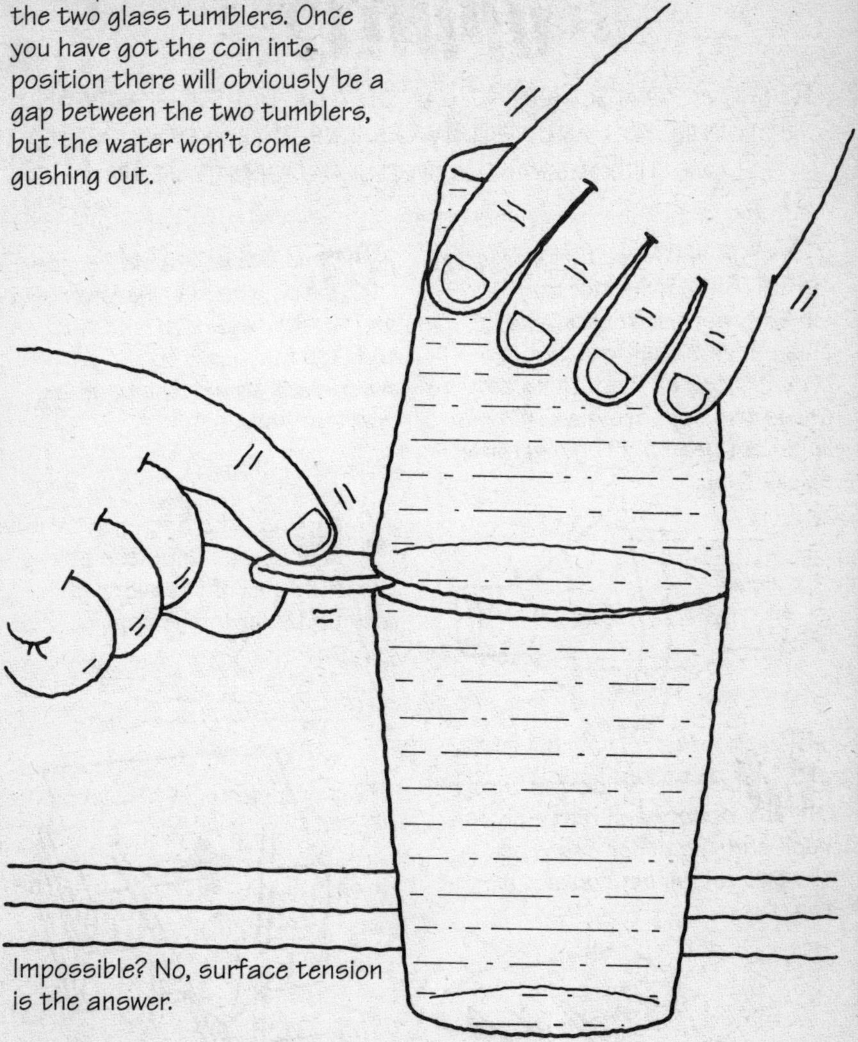

Impossible? No, surface tension is the answer.

The molecules that make up water tend to stick together and, provided you do not separate the glasses too much, the molecules will remain together and the water will not pour out.

# HOW CAN YOU ROLL UPHILL?

TO SHOW HOW SOMETHING CAN DEFY THE LAW OF GRAVITY AND ROLL UPHILL YOU WILL NEED: TWO STICKS, THREE BOOKS OF THE SAME THICKNESS AND A SPECIAL ANTI-GRAVITY ROLLER.

1 The anti-gravity roller is made from two cones joined together. You can make this out of cardboard, but probably the easiest thing to use is two tops from washing up liquid bottles held together with sticky tape.

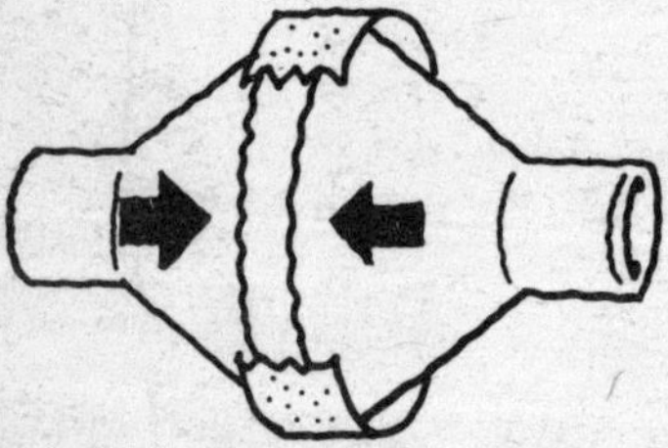

2 Place the sticks so that one end of each rests on one book and the other end rests on the two remaining books put together.

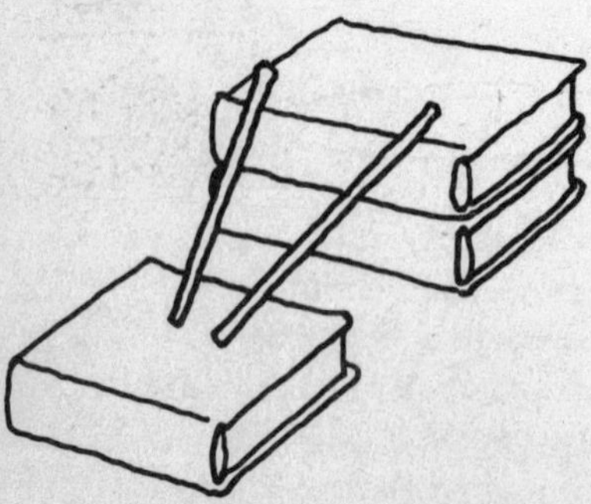

3 The sticks should be closer together at the lower end and further apart at the top end. You may have to experiment to get the position exactly right.

4 When the anti-gravity roller is rested on the sticks at the lower end of the slope it rolls up towards the top!

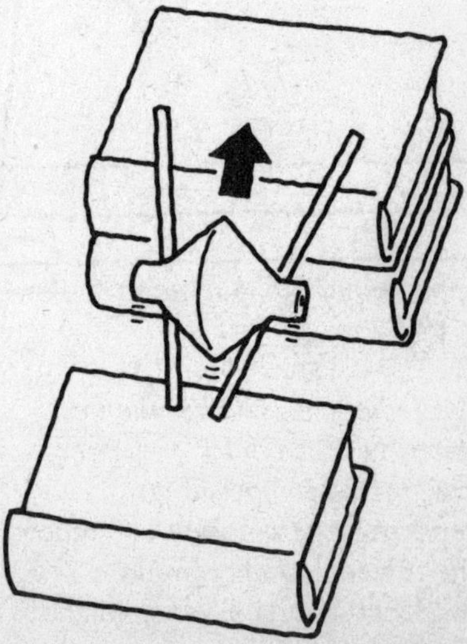

# HOW CAN YOU NEVER BE LOST AT SEA?

THANKS TO SATELLITES MODERN SAILORS NEED NEVER GET LOST.

All they need to find out exactly where they are is a simple device called a global satellite positioning system.

It's a sort of radio receiver which tunes into seventeen possible satellites orbiting earth some 11,000 miles above the surface.

Each satellite transmits signals giving the time of day and its relative position.

If the receiver gets a message from three or more satellites it works out how long the signal takes to come from each satellite and from this information it can calculate its exact position.

# HOW TO MAKE A FRIEND FEEL SILLY!

1 **P**ress one of the coins onto your friend's forehead.

2 **A**sk them to leave it there for a few seconds before shaking if off. Repeat this three times.

3 **A**fter a few goes, press just your thumb onto your friend's forehead (but pretend you are putting on another coin!)

4 **A**sk them to shake it off. Because their forehead is numb from the cold coins, they will try to shake off a coin that isn't there.

5 **L**et them look in the mirror and they will see there has been no coin on their forehead at all ... Your friend is guaranteed to feel silly.

# HOW TO LINK TWO PAPER-CLIPS WITHOUT TOUCHING THEM

**ALL YOU NEED** for this amazing feat are two paper-clips and a sheet of paper.

1. Fold one end of the paper over and push one of the clips over both layers of paper.

2. Now fold the other end of the paper in the opposite direction so it forms an 'S' shape. Place the second clip over the two layers of paper to the rear.

3. Show everyone the paper and the clips. The clips are definitely not linked at this point and you will not have to touch them to make them link.

4. Pull the ends of the paper apart sharply. The paper-clips will leap off the paper and link themselves together!

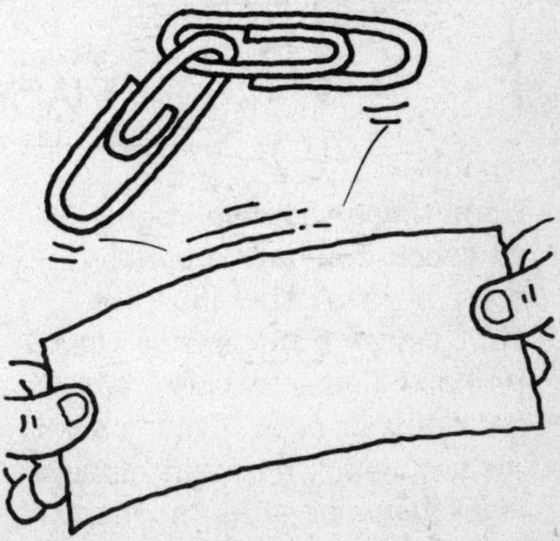

# HOW DO YOU GET RID OF HICCUPS?

Under your lungs there is a sheet of muscle called the diaphragm. This moves up and down as an important part of the breathing process. When it goes up it forces air out of your lungs, and when it goes down the lungs fill with air again.

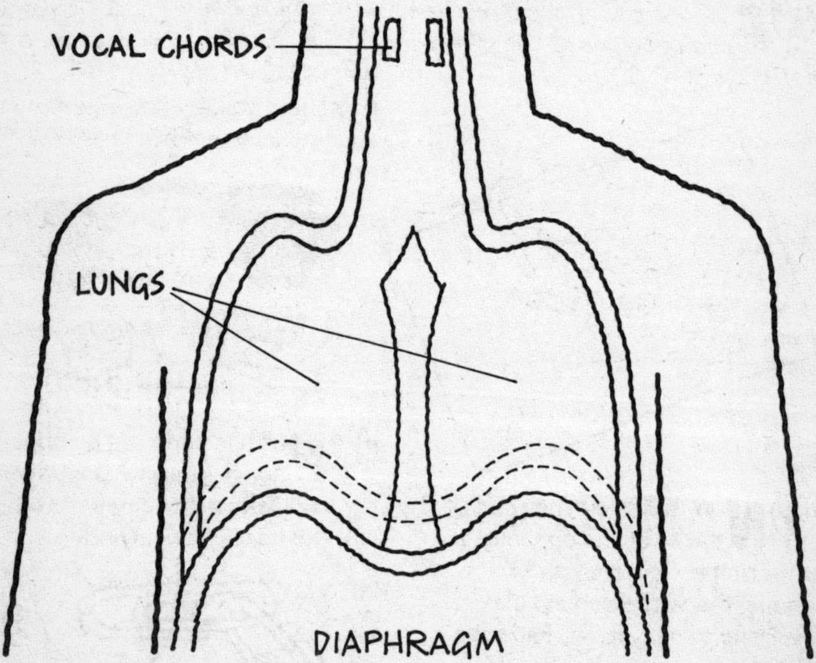


Sometimes the diaphragm twitches. You have probably come across other muscles that twitch from time to time – perhaps in your eyelid or at the back of your neck. This is called an involuntary muscular spasm – which means that the muscle has gone bananas!

When the diaphragm twitches it causes quick bursts of air to be drawn in and out of the lungs very quickly. As the air goes in and out of the vocal chords it slams them open and shut and creates the noise known as a hiccup.

But how do you stop them?

One popular cure is to stand on your head and drink a glass of water from the wrong side of the glass.

You could even try jumping up and down on the spot.

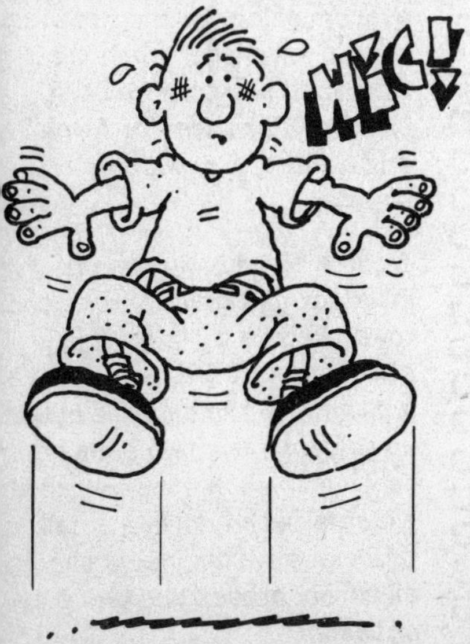


Or you could take a deep breath and get someone to drop a cold spoon down the back of your neck.

Perhaps if someone gave you a shock, scared you or made you jump that would do the trick?

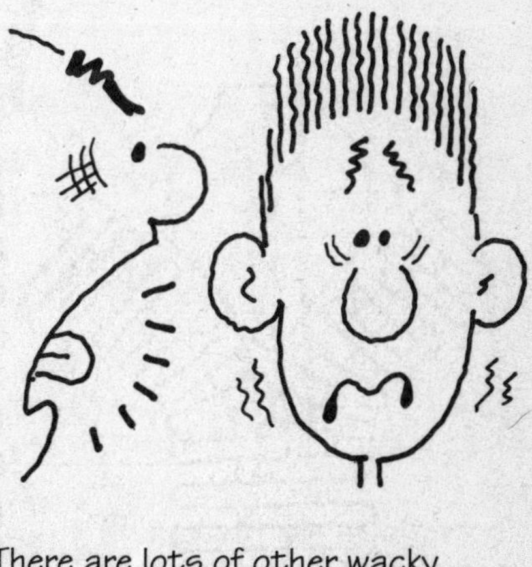

There are lots of other wacky cures but the truth is that most hiccups will go away on their own. The cure that suits you best is the one that suits you best. Try them all if you like, but if hiccups persist for a long time then you should see a doctor!

# HOW DOES A ZIP WORK?

THE ZIP WAS INVENTED IN 1891 BY WHITCOMB JUDSON, AN AMERICAN ENGINEER.

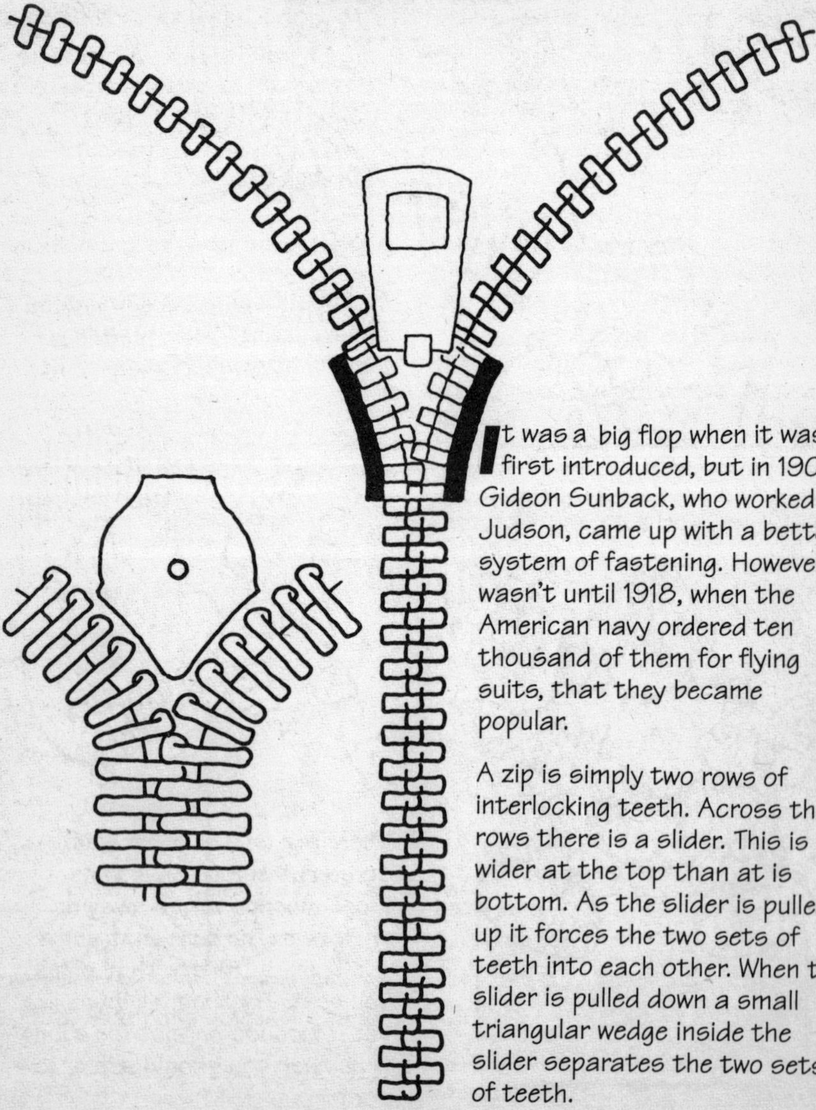

It was a big flop when it was first introduced, but in 1906 Gideon Sunback, who worked f Judson, came up with a better system of fastening. However, wasn't until 1918, when the American navy ordered ten thousand of them for flying suits, that they became popular.

A zip is simply two rows of interlocking teeth. Across the rows there is a slider. This is wider at the top than at is bottom. As the slider is pulled up it forces the two sets of teeth into each other. When th slider is pulled down a small triangular wedge inside the slider separates the two sets of teeth.

# HOW TO MAKE YOUR MARK

**ALL YOU NEED** for this fiendish prank is a coin, a sheet of paper, a soft leaded pencil – and a gullible friend.

1 **D**raw a cross on the paper and tell your friend that you are going to test his or her co-ordination.

2 **A**sk your victim to close his or her eyes and roll the coin down their forehead, over their nose, across their chin and then try to place it on the cross – still with his or her eyes closed.

3 **D**raw a ring around the coin to show where the coin was placed.

4 **N**ow ask your victim to have another go. Again mark the position of the coin by drawing around it with the pencil.

5 **A**fter a third attempt congratulate your friend on his or her brilliant co-ordination.

What he or she won't realise is that there is now a black line running down the centre of his or her face. Each time you draw around the coin some of the black goes onto the edge of the coin and it is then transferred to your friend's face.

# HOW DID A SHELL CREATE A FASHION?

In ancient times, Phoenecians found that they often got purple feet by walking on the beach. They discovered that this was caused by shells. These shells are called *murex* shells (or Murex trunculus if you want to be really clever and use the scientific name). They are about four centimetres long and a drab brown colour, but when crushed they produce a rich purple dye.

It was an amazing discovery, but unfortunately it took hundreds of shells to produce the dye in any quantity. And even then, it had to go through lots of different processes before it could be used for dying material. As a result the dye became very, very special. So special, in fact, that it was used only for the clothes of royalty.

Purple remained exclusive to royalty until the end of the 19th century. In 1856 William Henry Perkin, an eighteen-year-old laboratory assistant at the Royal College of Chemistry in London, found a way of producing purple dye without having to crush lots of shells. One day he got extremely frustrated with an experiment that kept going wrong. In a fit of frustration he threw all his chemicals into the sink. He was astonished to find, that when all the chemicals mixed together they turned a beautiful purple colour. Soon afterwards Britain's first dye manufacturing plant was set up and purple was no longer exclusive to royalty!

# HOW HIGH IS YOUR HOUSE?

HAVE YOU EVER WONDERED HOW HIGH YOUR HOUSE IS? YOU CAN EASILY FIND OUT – JUST BY LOOKING THROUGH YOUR LEGS!

1 First get a friend to stand still as you walk away from them, counting your steps as you go. Every so often, bend over and look back through your legs at your friend. Keep moving forwards until you can just see the top of your friend's head through your legs. Make a note of how many steps you had to take to get to that position.

2 Let's assume that you took six steps and that your friend is one and a half metres in height. It is just a simple question of arithmetic to assume that if you walked twelve steps away (twice the distance) you would be able to see the top of something twice as high as your friend.

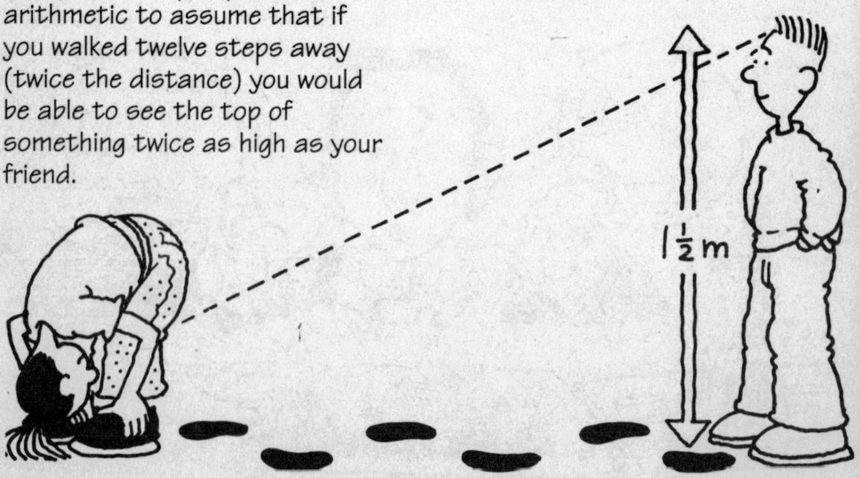

You can use this information to find out the height of your house.

3 Starting beside your house, walk away from it until you get to a position where you can just see the top of the house by looking back through your legs.

4 Keep a note of how many steps you took to get to that position. Divide the number of steps you have taken by the number of steps it took to see your friend's head. Multiply your answer by your friend's height. The answer you get from that multiplication is the height (more or less) of your house.

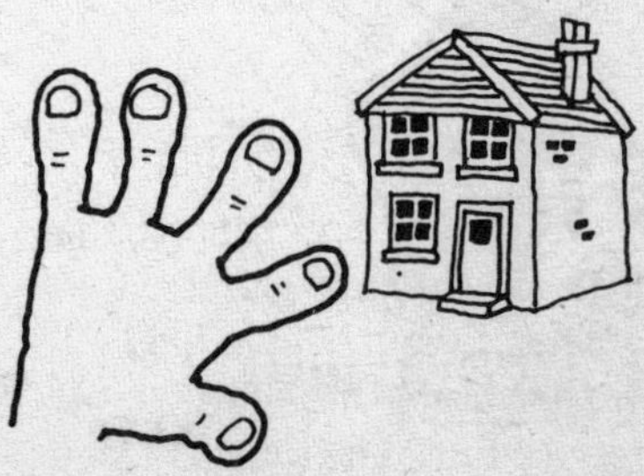

# HOW IS LEAD PUT INTO A PENCIL?

PENCILS ARE MADE IN MUCH THE SAME WAY THAT YOU WOULD MAKE A SANDWICH.

Instead of two slices of bread the pencil manufacturer uses two blocks of wood. Instead of butter or margarine, glue is used and the filling consists of rods of graphite or clay or wax (or a mixture in the case of coloured pencils).

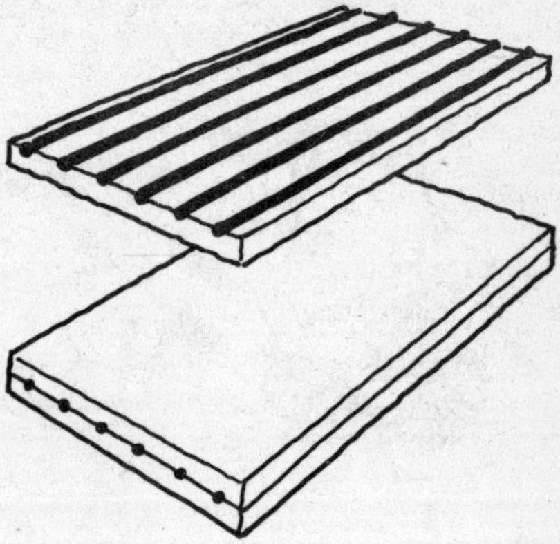

1 Pencils start off life as two pieces of flat wood. Grooves are cut in both pieces of wood.

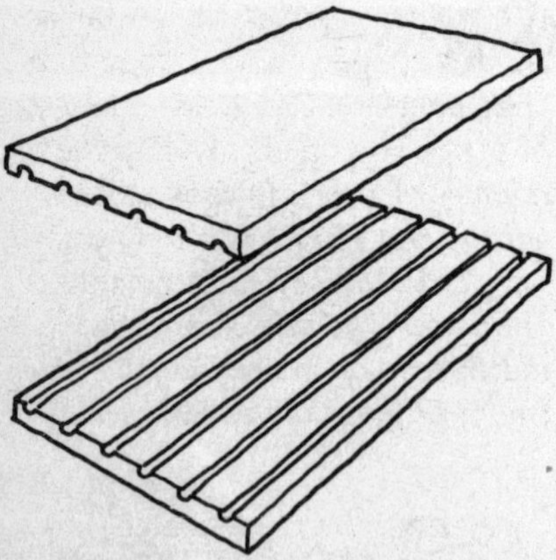

2 The leads are laid in the grooves and then the two pieces of wood are glued together. Everything is held together under massive pressure until the glue has set.

3 Grooves are now made in the top and bottom surface of the block and then the individual pencils are separated.

If you look at the end of a pencil you can see where the two pieces of wood have been joined together.

# HOW MESSY IS A HUMAN BEING?

YOU MAY THINK SOMEONE IS MESSY IF THEIR CLOTHES ARE DIRTY OR DISHEVELLED, OR IF THEIR ROOM IS UNTIDY, OR BECAUSE THEY DON'T WASH VERY OFTEN.

Believe it or not, the cleanest, tidiest, and most fastidious person is still pretty messy.

This is because we all shed skin. A lot of animals, such as snakes, shed their skins, but quite often this is done in one complete piece. This is done so that the animal can grow.

Surprisingly humans also shed skin. Not in one piece of course, but everyday skin gets rubbed off. The average human loses about 30 grammes of skin every day.

Most dust in a house is made up of human skin. When you are vacuuming you are really sucking up bits of your own family!

In a year the average human loses some eleven kilos of skin.

# HOW TO READ SOMEONE'S MIND

1 Place three coins on a table in front of a friend.

2 Turn your back and ask your friend to pick up any one of the three coins and hold it firmly in their fist.

3 Ask them to place the hand holding the coin up to their forehead and to concentrate on whether the coin was in the left, right or centre position when it was on the table. Tell them to keep concentrating. They are not concentrating hard enough. Tell them to concentrate even harder.

4 Now ask them to place the coin back on the table in its original position.

5 When this has been done, turn round and place your left hand against your friend's forehead. You now read his or her mind and tell him or her which coin they took.

How do you know? Well as you reach forward to touch your friend's forehead casually rest your other hand on the three coins. You will know immediately which coin has been chosen because (having been in your friend's hand for a while) it will be the warmest of the three.

# HOW DO YOU MARBLE?

MARBLING IS A SIMPLE BUT EFFECTIVE AND VERY ATTRACTIVE WAY OF DECORATING PAPER.

**ALL YOU NEED** is a tray of water, some oil paint, a stick and some plain paper.

1. Squeeze some oil paint onto the surface of the water. You can use ordinary powder paint, but if you do this you should also add some cooking-oil because the paint has to be oil based.

2. Use the stick to stir the paint from side to side. Depending upon what sort of design you want, you can add others colours to the water if you want.

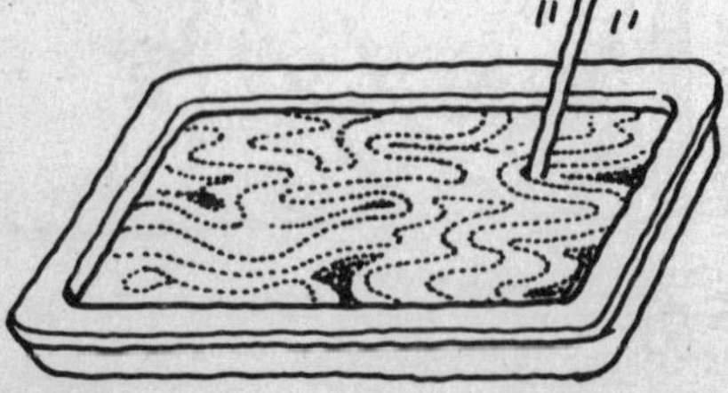

3. Drop a sheet of paper on top of the water and leave it there for a few seconds.

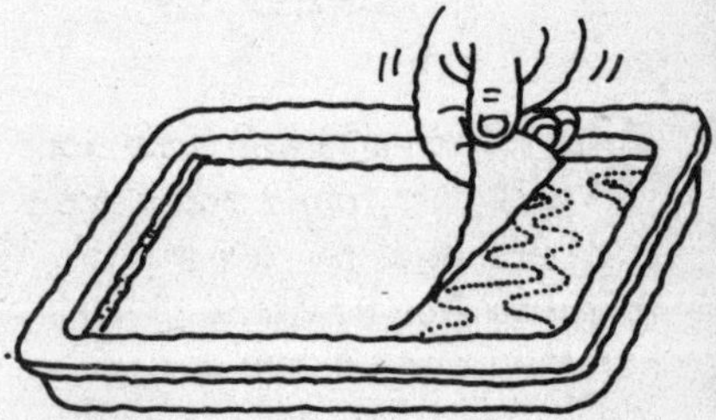

4. Lift the paper off and then hang it up to dry – be careful where the drips fall!

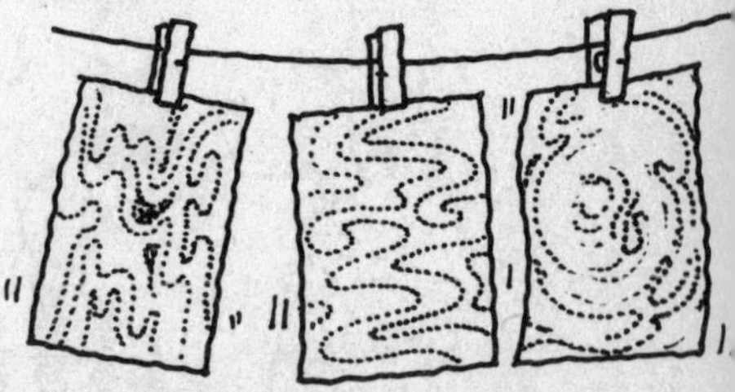

When the paper is dry you can use it to wrap gifts, cover books or even frame it to make an attractive abstract picture for your room.

# HOW CAN ONE RUBBER LIFT TWENTY?

AS WELL AS 21 RUBBERS YOU ALSO NEED SOME STRING, A COTTON-REEL AND A SMALL BAG.

1 Place 20 rubbers in the bag. Tie the neck of the bag to one end of the string.

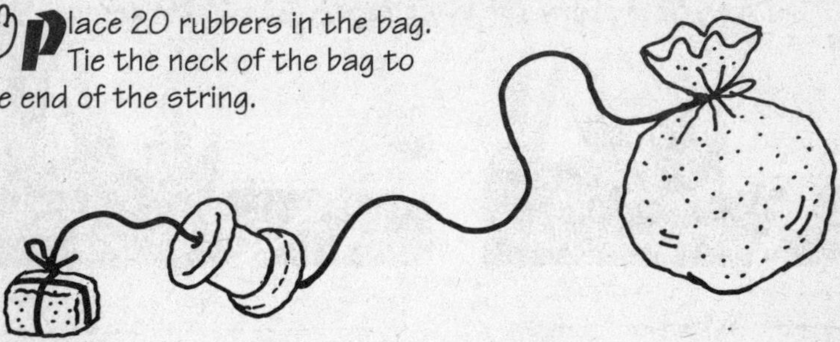

2 Thread the other end of the string through the cotton-reel and then tie the single rubber to it.

3 Now hold the cotton reel in one hand and start the rubber at the top spinning around on the end of its string.

4 As you swing the rubber, centrifugal force causes it to move outwards further and further away from the cotton reel. This pulls the string up and as a result the bag of rubbers is lifted also.

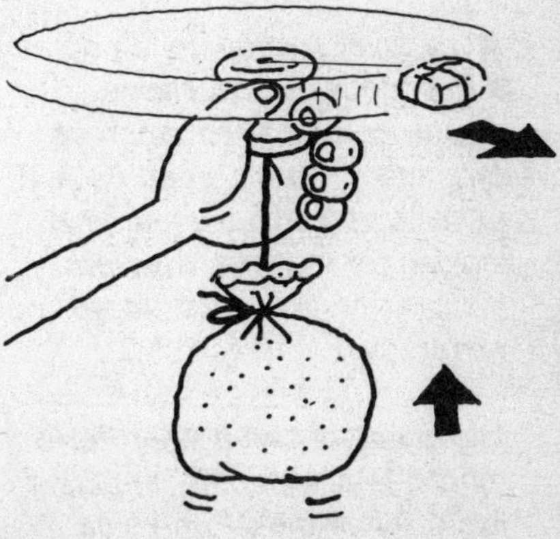

So one rubber has managed to lift the other twenty!

# HOW DOES AN ARCHER FISH SHOOT ITS SUPPER?

THE ARCHER FISH IS THE ROBIN HOOD OF THE WATER WORLD. IT CAN SHOOT ITS PREY FROM AS FAR AWAY AS 3½ METRES.

It is a very small fish that lives in coastal areas, river estuaries and the mangrove swamps of south-east Asia. It patrols beneath the surface looking for insects that are climbing on branches above the water.

The inside of the archer fish's mouth is arranged something like a water pistol and this enables the fish to squirt droplets of water at its target.

The archer fish is very accurate with its shooting because it has to compensate for the fact that water bends light. Because of this, the insect is not actually where the archer fish can see it and the fish has to allow for this difference when it fires its water.

The water stuns the insect, the insect drops into the water and the archer fish has got its supper.

# HOW TO CLEAN SILVER WITH KITCHEN FOIL

1 Place a sheet of kitchen (aluminium) foil, or some foil milk-bottle tops, into a bowl or an old jar.

2 Dissolve some washing-soda crystals in warm water and pour this on top of the foil.

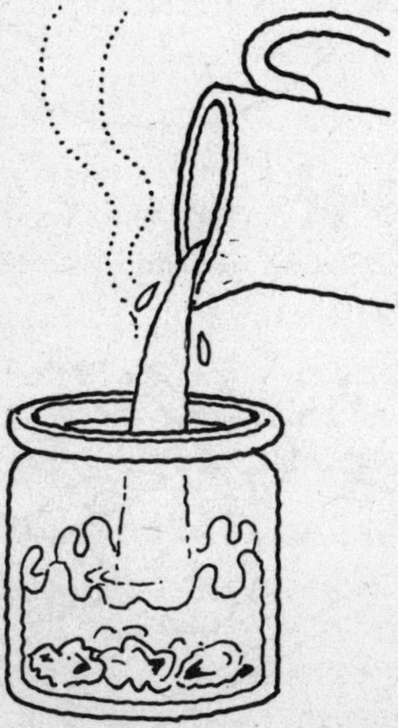

3 Now put your dirty silver into the water, on top of the foil (wear rubber gloves when you do this).

After a few seconds, bubbles will appear on the silver. A chemical reaction has started between the two metals, the aluminium and the silver. The tarnish is removed from the silver, travels through the water and attaches itself to the foil.

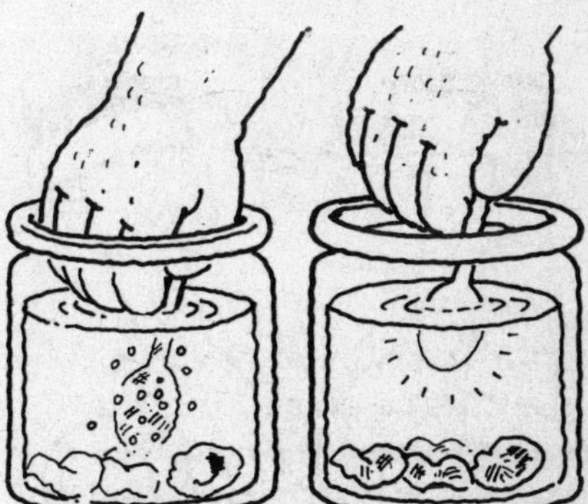

After an hour or so the silver will be extremely clean and the aluminium will be tarnished.

If you use this system to clean cutlery, make sure that you rinse the cutlery very well before using it to eat.

# HOW CAN YOU EAT A STAINED-GLASS WINDOW?

BEFORE YOU CAN EAT YOUR STAINED GLASS WINDOW YOU HAVE TO MAKE IT.

**YOU WILL NEED:** 6 oz of plain flour, 3 oz of margarine, a pinch of salt, some water and some boiled sweets.

1. **P**ut the flour and salt into a bowl. Cut the fat into small cubes and then use your hands to rub it into the flour until you have a mixture that resembles breadcrumbs.

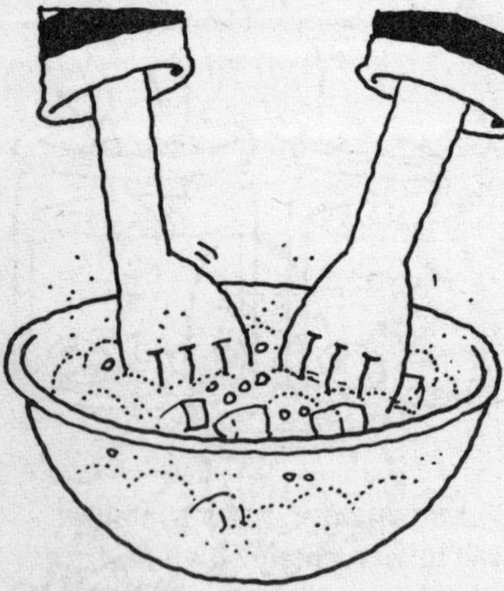

2. **M**ake a 'well' in the centre of the mixture and pour in a small amount of water. Mix this in and then add more water. When the mixture sticks together and you can squeeze it into one lump you have added enough water.

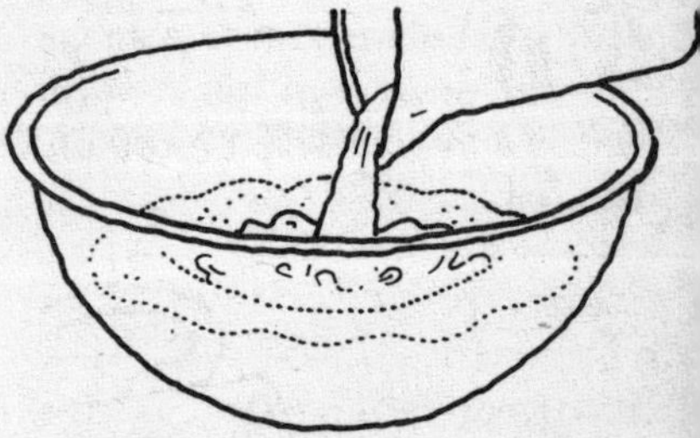

3. **R**oll out the pastry on a surface that you have previously dusted with some flour.

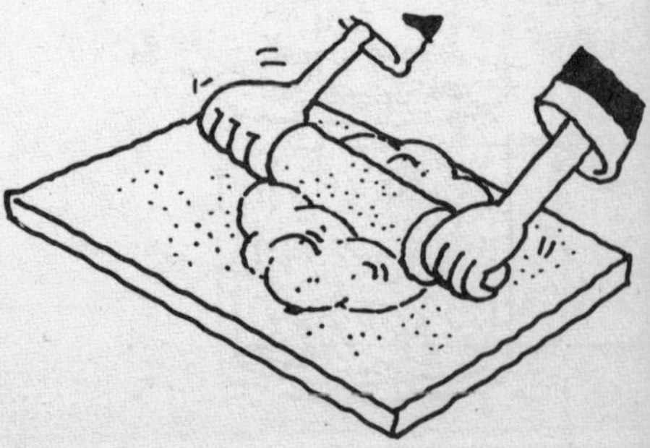

4 Now cut out the shape you want for your stained glass window. You can have any shape you like, perhaps the drawings on this page will give you some ideas.

5 To make the 'glass' for your stained-glass window you need to crush the boiled sweets. Put the sweets in a strong plastic bag and bash them on a hard surface, with a hammer. Make sure that you don't hit your fingers!

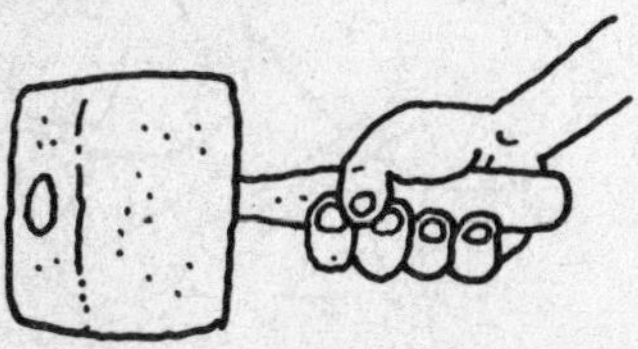

6 Pour some of the broken sweets into each of the window shapes you cut into the pastry. You can mix the colours in each window to make it more attractive if you wish.

Now comes the exciting bit. This is when you cook your stained glass window. Place the tray in a pre-heated oven at 425 degrees F/220 degrees C/ Gas Mark 7, for 15 to 20 minutes.

7 When you take it out of the oven you will find that the pastry has cooked and the sweets have melted. The boiled sweets will be extremely hot, so be very careful how you handle your window. Allow it to cool and you have a beautiful stained glass window.

Hold it up to the light and you will be able to appreciate what a wonderful work of art you have created. Not only that, you can eat it as well!

# HOW TO LIFT AN ICE-CUBE WITH A MATCHSTICK!

1 Show your friends an ice-cube and a matchstick and challenge them to pick up the ice-cube with the match.

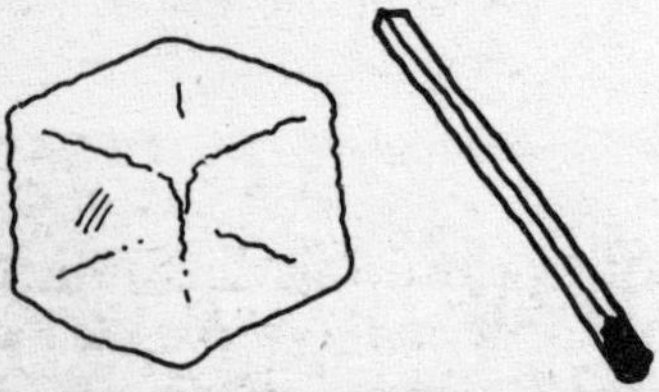

2 When they give up, lay the matchstick on top of the ice-cube.

3 Pour some salt onto the ice-cube and over the centre of the match.

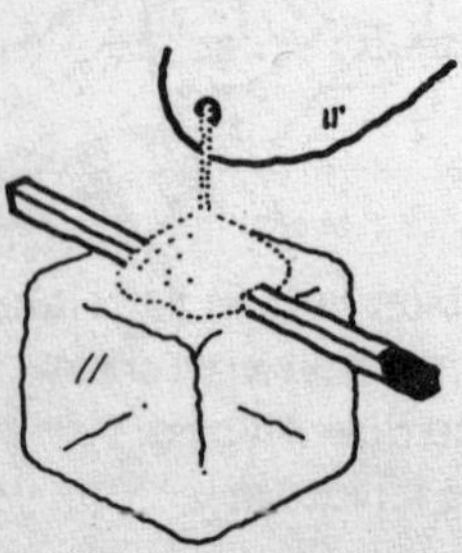

4 The salt causes the ice to melt and then absorbs som of the water formed. If the ice-cube is cold enough the water then refreezes around the matchstick.

5 Now all you have to do is hol each end of the match and lift . . . and the matchstick lifts the ice-cube!

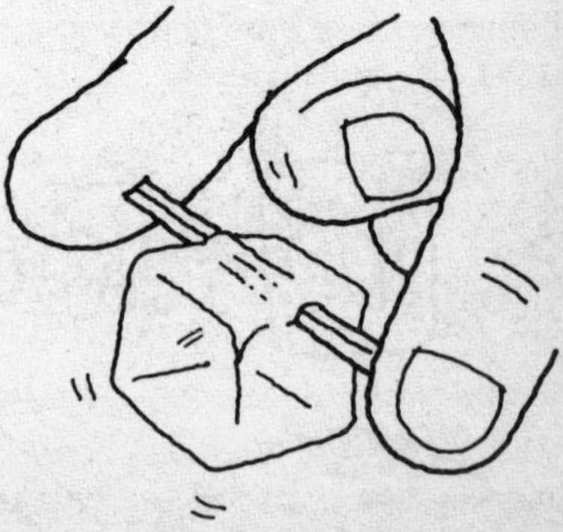

Remember never to play with live matches!

# HOW CAN A WORM HELP A REFUSE COLLECTOR?

THE AVERAGE FAMILY PRODUCES A TON OF RUBBISH EVERY YEAR.

But there is a lot of stuff we can recycle. Bottles can be taken to bottle banks, cans to a can bank and newspapers and comics can be made into recycled paper.

A major problem with household rubbish has always been the disposal of food-waste. If you just leave it to rot it produces a rather stinky gas, called methane. This is where a worm can help out.

The tiger worm loves to chomp its way through food-waste. Put some of these worms in a container, called a wormery, and throw all your vegetables and food-waste in on top of them. It takes 200 tiger worms to gobble up the 2½kg (5½lb) of food waste that the average family of four throws away each week.

The worms make a rich, dry compost which is excellent for the garden. The worms also produce a liquid which is collected at the bottom of the wormery. This is full of nutrients and can be collected and poured on plants.

The more stuff we recycle the less there will be for the dustmen to carry away. And that is how a worm can help a refuse collector.